Patchwork
Made Easy

For Tess, Nick and Paul

MILNER CRAFT SERIES

Patchwork Made Easy

Quick modern methods for traditional quilts

Rosemary Donoughue Schaer

SALLY MILNER PUBLISHING

First published in 1991 by
Sally Milner Publishing Pty Ltd
PO Box 2104
Bowral NSW 2576
AUSTRALIA

Relaunched 2000

Photography by Werner Langer
Layout by Doric Order

Printed in Hong Kong

National Library of Australia
Cataloguing-in-Publication data:

Donoughue Schaer, Rosemary
Patchwork made easy

ISBN 1 86351 253 5.

1. Patchwork quilts. 2. Patchwork. 1. Title.
(Series: Milner craft series

746.46

ACKNOWLEDGEMENTS

Several quilters stayed up till all hours of the night and neglected their families in order to finish quilts for this book. My thanks to Alyson Crawford, Carmel Ellis, Sue Gill, Pam Hendy, Gal McLellan, Susan Manderson, Ros Miller, Ailsa Mills, Denise Nielsen, Sharon Pick, Maryann Rowland and young Jackson Turner for lending their quilts, and in particular to Robyn Parry and Anne Whitsed who made quilts especially for this book. Many of the quilters were beginners, and their efforts are to be congratulated.

This book would never have come about had I not first tutored many students in these methods at Patchwork Supplies in Brisbane. I am very grateful to Ruth Stonley for giving me that opportunity and for her encouragement.

Rosemary Donoughue Schaer, 2000

CONTENTS

INTRODUCTION

There's a popular image of quilters as little old ladies who cut up well-worn clothes and laboriously piece together small hexagons to make knee rugs.

We're not all like that! Some of us *may* admit to being small, but certainly not old, and the quilts we make range from simple cot quilts in traditional designs to contemporary works of art which hang in public buildings. Quilters make their works for all sorts of reasons, not just to put covers on beds, but to express their own personality and creativity, to help them through bad times and as an outlet for the pressures of everyday living, and to celebrate good times, friendship and happy occasions.

Since the resurgence of interest in patchwork and quilting over the past twenty or so years there have been enormous developments, in both the areas of design and techniques. The introduction in recent years of a wide variety of tools to facilitate the rapid piecing of certain types of quilts has been probably the greatest revolution in the craft of quiltmaking since the invention of the sewing machine in the 1860s. For some it has enabled the more rapid production of traditional designs, for others it has inspired experimentation to produce more contemporary artistic statements.

The speed piecing methods in this book concentrate on traditional designs, most of which have seen their most successful expression in the quilts of the Amish people of North America, whose use of colour and superb workmanship have made these quilts collectors' items. Because of the tradition from which these quilts spring, some people may regard the use of speed piecing techniques and tools as a contradiction — not traditional and therefore not the 'right' way to go about patchwork. I don't worry too much about these remarks. Much the same comments were made about machine-piecing when the sewing machine first came into use, and are still being made about the superiority of hand-piecing over machine-piecing. Yet many of the heirloom quilts so highly prized and sought after today, were quite probably the products of early machine-piecing. I doubt whether these purists do their hand sewing by candlelight or oil lamp, nor visit their quilt shop by horse and buggy! Times and manners change, and I'm sure the pioneer women would have leapt at the chance to use a rotary fabric cutter if it had been available. I believe that equal care and workmanship can be put into a quilt using modern tools. Most of us are not making quilts for competition, to be judged down to the last stitch. A quilt is an expression of our own artistic and creative aspirations and, above all, something to enjoy. If you don't enjoy piecing by template, hand stitching or quilting twenty stitches to the inch, you don't need to.

If you have already learnt other methods of piecing patchwork quilts, this book is not asking you to abandon them. There is an enormous amount of patchwork that cannot employ these methods, that *must* be done by more traditional means. Yet speed piecing has a place, even for quilters (like myself!) who do enjoy piecing by template or hand sewing. It is just another skill, to be utilised where appropriate.

Even if you have never considered using these methods before, they are worth considering if:

- the quilt is for a child's bed (do you want to see peanut butter smeared on a quilt that took you three years to make?)
- you love quilting but don't enjoy piecing a quilt
- the quilt is to give away (*and* it has to be completed by the week after next!)
- the quilt is for a raffle, to raise funds for a school, etc.
- you just don't have time to make a traditionally pieced quilt for each of your ten children!
- you are a beginner, and would like a gentle introduction into the art of quiltmaking.

The quilt patterns in this book are the product of a series of workshops I have been conducting over the past eleven years, and as such are well tested. It all began with a Trip Around the World workshop to raise funds for our kindergarten, but I was soon being asked to run more workshops. It appeared there were many more women who had the desire but not the time to make traditional patchwork quilts. Their sewing skills ranged from the very competent down to those who admitted to being afraid of their sewing machines! The only pre-requisite is being able to sew a (reasonably!) straight line.

MATERIALS

1) FABRICS

The most important choice for your quilt is the choice of fabrics and plenty of thought should go into this. Study the colour plates for ideas of colour combinations, and try to visualise as you choose just *how much of each colour* will appear in the quilt. Ensure there is sufficient contrast where it is needed (e.g. on opposite sides of the Log Cabin blocks, or the different 'chains' in Double or Triple Irish Chains) while maintaining an overall blending of colours. Many quilters will nominate fabric choice as the hardest part of any patchwork project.

Choosing six or seven coordinating fabrics for a quilt can be difficult. A good way to start is to find one fabric you really like, say a floral, which has a lot of different colours in it. Examine these colours carefully and find other fabrics to match them. You should, if using print fabrics, have a variety of sizes of prints — small, medium and large — and perhaps some plains or monotones (monotone prints will often appear plain from a distance). Stand back from your fabrics when choosing. If you are to use all plain fabrics in the quilt, you may like to grade it through various shades of two or three colours.

Plain fabrics will show up hand quilting better than print fabrics, so take this into account when choosing fabrics — don't add plain borders if you hate hand quilting, and don't waste an intricately quilted feather wreath on a print!

Some mention should also be made of stripes, checks and placement prints. The nature of the strip piecing techniques used here is such that fabrics may not be placed in each square or diamond exactly as you would choose if cutting them by template. Checks may disappear off the edge of a patch, and stripes may go in various directions. This is not necessarily something to avoid, but to be aware of.

The purists will tell you that patchwork must all be done using 100% cottons. While cotton is certainly lovely to work with, I see no reason not to introduce poly-cottons or even silks and other fabrics if they create the desired effect. Just be aware that some of these fabrics may be difficult to handle (silk frays badly, poly-cottons have very little 'give') and a quilt pieced in a variety of fabrics may not piece together quite as smoothly at times as one pieced with the same fabric throughout, be it cottons, poly-cottons, silks or whatever. You may encounter some problems with tension or puckering where different fabrics join, or you may not. The extra stretch in cotton can be useful if you have to manipulate it to make it fit, a little 'fudging' can be preferable to re-sewing. Don't avoid other fabrics, just be aware of their different properties. After all, even cottons can vary in density, elasticity, colour fastness, etc. from one manufacturer to another.

All fabrics must be washed and ironed separately before use. The importance of this cannot be over-emphasised. Even the most unlikely colours will run. It is tragic to find your beautifully pieced patchwork mottled with dye after the first wash! Wash fabrics in the same manner as you will later wash the quilt — cold or warm water, with your usual detergent (dissolve well *before* adding fabric).

Most fabrics today are at least 106 cm (42 inches) wide and up to 120 cm (47 inches) wide, and all instructions and fabric requirements have been based on this premise. Narrower fabrics may be used, but fabric requirements will have to be increased accordingly, and you will have to cut extra strips. They can be a bit of a nuisance in the Trip Around the World quilt.

2) ROTARY FABRIC CUTTERS, MATS AND RULERS

These three pieces of equipment are essential for the speed piecing techniques outlined in this book (with the possible exception of the Amish Basket Quilt). Having mastered their use you will find you can utilise them in all sorts of other projects, and therefore you should aim to purchase the best you can afford.

There are a few **rotary cutters** on the market, the best known being Olfa and Kaicut. The choice comes down to personal preference, and if you get the opportunity to try out the various types before buying, it is wise to do so. The Olfa cutter comes in three sizes – I find the medium one more comfortable to use, but again, this is a personal thing. The Kaicut cutter has the advantage of a blade that retracts automatically after use. This is a safety advantage, but it requires a little more pressure for cutting. Replacement blades are available for all the cutters, but are relatively expensive, and it pays to take care of the blades. Keep your cutter away from damp places, occasionally place a drop of oil between the blade and the nut and, above all, never cut paper, run over pins, scrape your blade along the edge of the ruler, or cut on anything but the soft, self healing cutting mats made for the purpose.

There are also several **cutting mats** available on the market. Here, more than anywhere, the rule of 'buy the best you can afford' applies, 'the best' being (a) as big as possible, and (b) one with grid lines marked on it. A very small mat with no grid on it is next to useless — it is almost impossible to fold the fabric small enough to fit on the mat, and the lack of grid lines makes cutting inaccurate.

Boards are available from art supply shops as well as quilting shops. However make sure your board has measurements marked in Imperial measurements (inches) not metric (see below).

Grid lines are essential on the cutting board for accurately folding and trimming fabric before cutting strips. Some boards also have 45° and 60° angles marked on them — the former is useful for the Lone Star Quilt.

If you already have a cutting mat which has no grid lines marked on it, you may be able to add your own using a permanent felt pen. Use a large set square or carpenter's square to ensure accurate 90° angles. If your cutting board has no 45° angles marked on it, you may wish to add one before making the Lone Star Quilt.

Take care not to leave your cutting mat anywhere it is exposed to the sun, as it will warp badly. This is particularly relevant if you travel to workshops by car.

The **quilters rulers**, which are thick, see-through rulers with strip-width markings, are basically available in two widths — 3-inch-wide and 6-inch-wide. The 6-inch rulers are fairly heavy and perhaps a little cumbersome, but their weight is an advantage in holding the fabric firmly while cutting. The 6-inch rulers are also available in a shorter length, but these are not recommended for cutting long strips of fabric, as in these instructions. The 3-inch ruler is a little easier to handle, but obviously does not cater for wide strip piecing. As with the cutters and boards, the choice is very personal, and it is useful if you can try other people's first, before making a decision!

You will notice that most of the equipment available is in Imperial measurements (inches). This is because it either comes from, or caters for, the US market. Most books which deal with strip piecing (including this one) must therefore work on Imperial measurements. There are both boards and rulers which are marked in metric measurements (centimetres). The boards are really no different to use from those marked in Imperial, but metric rulers bear no relationship to the majority of instructions available for strip piecing. There is at least one ruler which has both metric and Imperial measurements, but I find the sheer quantity of lines on it is confusing.

TECHNIQUES

Take time to become comfortable and confident in using your rotary cutter before attempting any of the projects in this book. Practice on some scrap fabric at least four layers thick until you feel you can guide the cutter accurately and you are cutting through all the layers in a single stroke of the blade.

Set your cutting mat up on a table at a comfortable height. You need to be able to press down on the cutter as you work, so a dining table is a better height than a kitchen bench. Always *cut away from you,* not towards you or from side to side. This is both safer, and allows more even pressure on the blade, as well as greater accuracy in following the edge of the ruler.

Hold the ruler down firmly with your left-hand (all instructions are for right-handers — left-handers should reverse everything, but they're probably used to doing that!). You will need to keep pretty firm pressure on it so that it doesn't move when you're cutting. Keep your fingers away from the right-hand edge!

Hold the cutter adjacent to the right-hand side of the ruler. (The blade side of the cutter should always be next to the ruler). Press down firmly on the cutter until you feel it go through all the layers of fabric and reach the board (don't be afraid to apply pressure — it won't harm the cutter). Once you're sure you are through all the layers, roll the cutter away from you — keep it against the ruler, angling it in just slightly so it won't go off at a tangent. Hold the ruler firmly or it might slip aside, and don't stop cutting until you reach the end of the fabric. You should be able to cut your fabric with one stroke — avoid 'sawing' backwards and forwards — it will fray the edges of the fabric. If the cut has not gone through all the layers, you have not applied enough pressure. If one or two threads have been missed at regular intervals, it may mean you have a nick in the blade.

By now you will be aware of how sharp the rotary cutter is, and therefore how *dangerous!* Keep it away from children, and unless yours has an automatically retracting blade, always, always, *always* push the cover closed after every cut. This should become second nature to you when using it. Even bumping your fingers on an unsheathed blade can result in several stitches, and dropping one on your foot, or your child, doesn't bear thinking about!

I will now explain the techniques for cutting and piecing strips of fabric which form the basics for most of the quilts in this book.

For any strip piecing, the strips cut from the fabrics *must* be straight, and the following instructions are aimed at ensuring that. Make sure you are familiar with these techniques before beginning any of the projects in this book.

To begin with, you must ensure you have a perfectly straight edge from which to begin cutting. All strips are cut horizontally across the fabric, so it is the raw cut edge which must be trimmed.

Begin by folding the fabric in half down its length, following as closely as possible the grain of the fabric (the warp, or lengthwise grain of a fabric is usually pretty straight). Lay this folded edge along one of the horizontal lines near the top of your cutting board (Figure A).

Now fold the bottom edge (selvedges) of the fabric up so that this fold also follows one of the horizontal lines, at the bottom of the cutting board (Figure B).

Line up the right-hand edge of your ruler with one

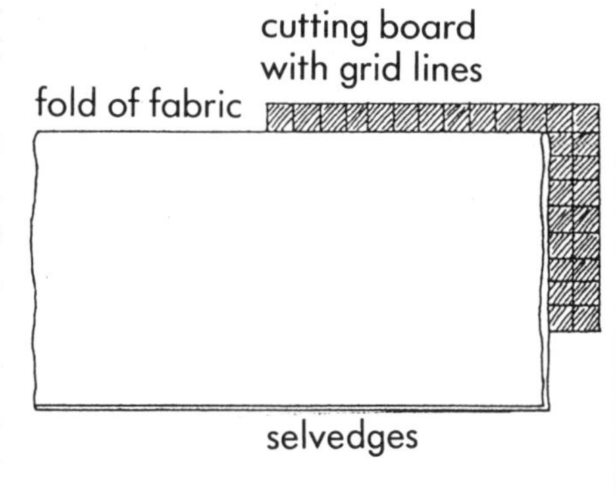

Figure A

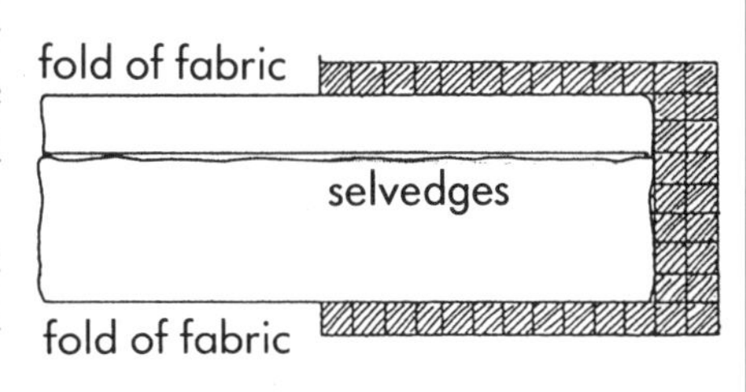

Figure B

of the vertical lines on the board closest to the raw edge of the fabric (Figure C) and trim off the raw edge.

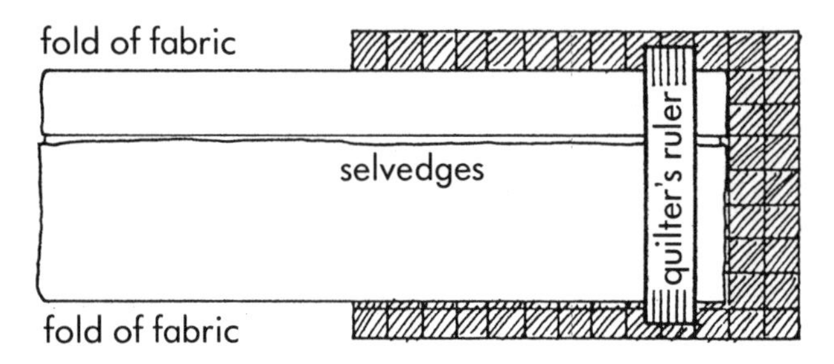

Figure C

This initial trimming-up is very important to ensure you have a straight edge to work from, and will be repeated again and again throughout the piecing process. After this initial trimming-up, check that you have folded and cut correctly by opening out the folds slightly — if there is a dip or a hump on the foldline, you will have to trim again (Figure D).

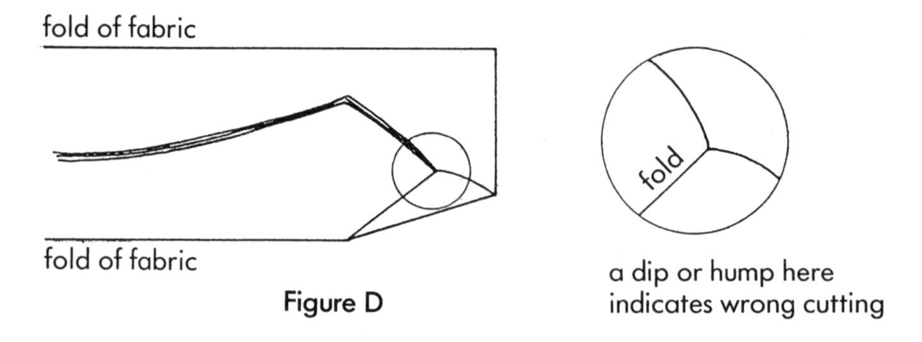

Figure D

a dip or hump here indicates wrong cutting

If you continue to cut wrongly, you will end up with strips of fabric that look like this (Figure E). It is impossible to sew these together and still end up with a flat quilt top!

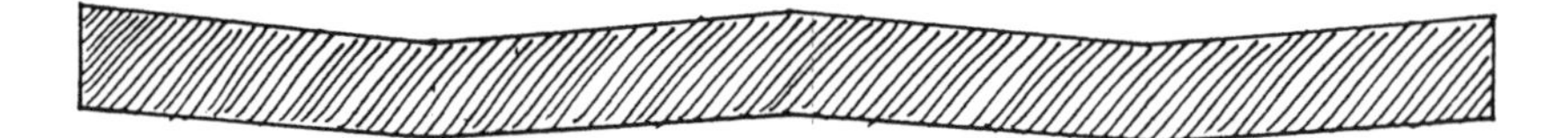

Figure E

Once you have successfully trimmed off the raw edge of your fabric, turn the whole thing around — board, cutter and all — so that the bulk of fabric is now on your right (left-handers, remember you will be doing the opposite!) (Figure F).

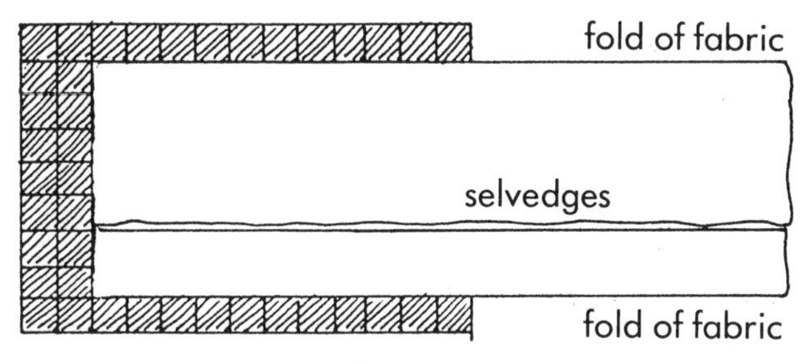

Figure F

You will now be using the inch-strip markings on your ruler as your cutting guide.

Place your ruler so that the line indicating the size of strip you want (e.g. 2½ inches) is on the trimmed edge of the fabric. (The ruler should be lying with the smaller measurements (½ inch, 1 inch, etc.) *on* the fabric and the larger measurements (3 inch, etc.) *outside* the fabric) (Figure G).

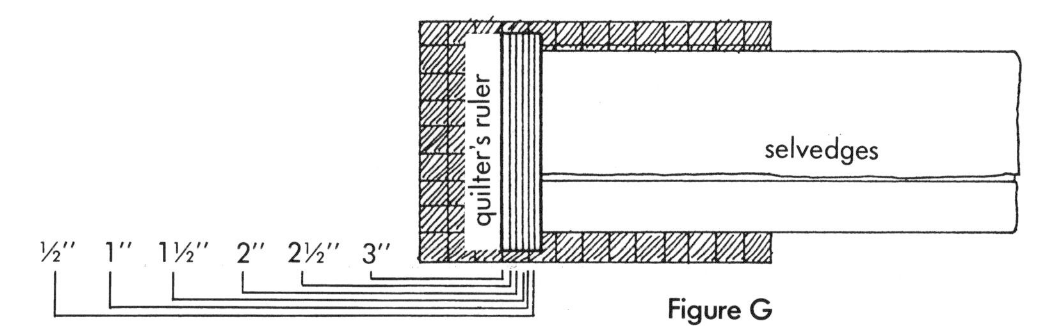

Figure G

Cut along the right-hand edge of the ruler, according to the initial instructions. You have cut your first strip! Keep two things in mind when cutting strips of fabric in this manner. Firstly, each strip should be checked for dips or humps as you did when you first trimmed up the fabric and, secondly, you will probably have to re-trim the end after every 5-6 cuts, as movement in the fabric will gradually throw it off-square. By regularly checking the strips as you cut them, you should be aware just when the fabric will need re-trimming.

In the first three chapters of the book, strips of fabric cut in this manner will be joined together in set sequences to form units of 3-7 strips. These units will then be cut in the opposite direction and rearranged to form the quilt designs. This is the basis of Seminole piecing, an invention of the Seminole Indians of North America, from which these methods derive.

Once these units of strips are made up and are being re-cut, you will probably have to trim up the end more frequently, possibly after each strip is cut. This is because the seams in the unit will cause it to distort more than a single piece of fabric. This becomes particularly noticeable in the Lone Star quilt, where the re-cutting of the strip-pieced unit is done at a 45° angle, creating a bias edge which is very fluid. Distortion of the units may be avoided somewhat if each successive strip is sewn from the opposite direction. Re-cutting of units is done with a single thickness of fabric only.

The piecing instructions in this book, and for most patchwork, use a ¼ inch/6 mm seam allowance. On most modern sewing machines, this is the distance between the needle and the right-hand edge of the pressure foot. Check your machine, and if this is the case, you will simply use your pressure foot as a seam guide. Some of the older machines, however, have wider feet, and you will have to work out, using a ruler or tape measure, just where the ¼ inch/6 mm line is and devise a means of following it. There may be some marking on the throat plate which you can follow, or you may wish to stick a piece of masking tape down

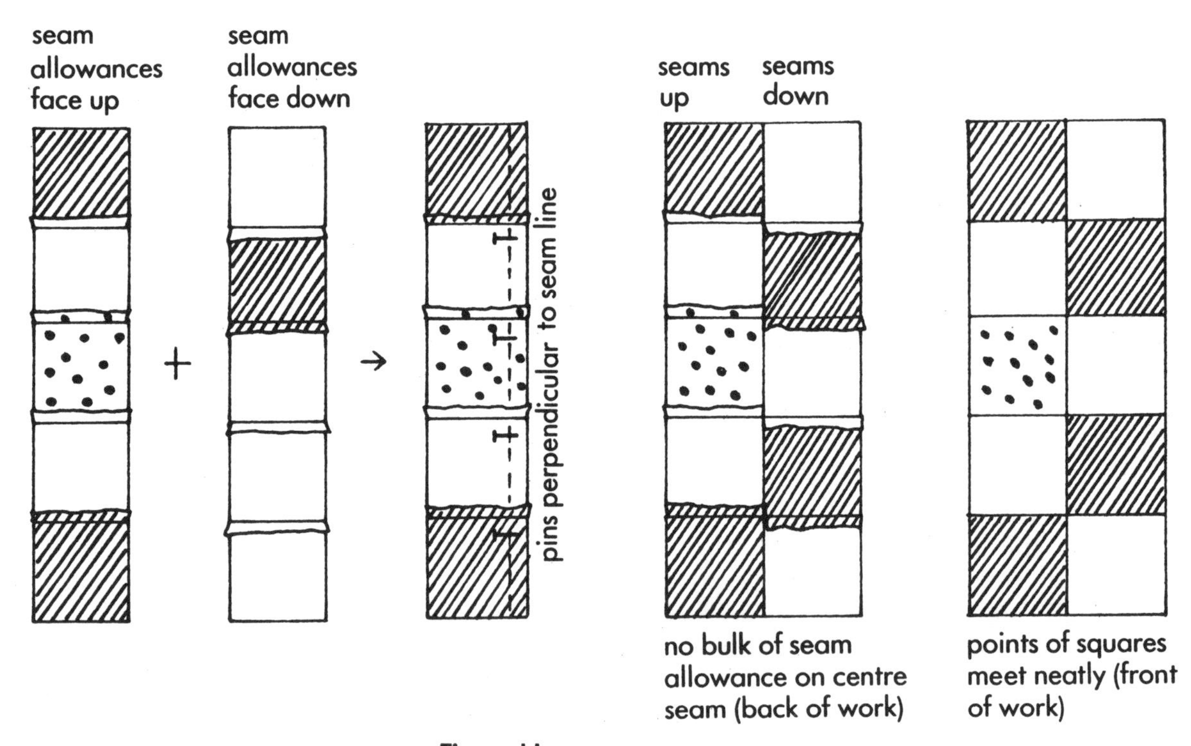

Figure H

on the throat plate as a seam guide. It is most important to be able to sew an accurate ¼ inch/6 mm seam, as all measurements are based around this and in some cases (e.g. the Irish Chain Quilts) your blocks will not join together accurately if you do not adhere to it.

Another technique worth mastering is *butted seams*. When strips from one-pieced unit are joined to strips from another pieced unit they should be placed so that their respective seam allowances face in opposite directions (this is always mentioned in the instructions). The purpose of this is (a) to reduce bulk where two seam allowances meet, and (b) to ensure the points of the patchwork patches meet up neatly. The ridge that forms on a seam when its seam allowance is pressed back helps it to 'lock into' the ridge on an adjoining seam. Place pins just below each of these intersections when joining these strips, only removing the pin when your machine needle has actually reached the intersection. Pinning should always be done with points towards the edge of the fabric (Figure H).

All seam allowances in patchwork are pressed to one side rather than open. The reason for this is not only to facilitate the 'butted seam' technique above, but to avoid any possibility of the quilt batting coming up through a loose seam onto the face of the quilt.

Some Notes About The Instructions

As mentioned earlier, these instructions have been used in the workshop for the past eleven years, and have been altered and modified to cater for most eventualities (what one of my students described as 'idiot-proofed'). All measurements [e.g. fabric requirements, number of strips to cut (Log Cabin), length of strips for piecing (Trip Around the World), number of pieced units required (Chapters 1, 2 and 3)] allow a margin for error, but are not wasteful of fabric. Each chapter contains instructions for a specific sized quilt, then a section on varying the size from the example quilt. Sometimes detailed fabric requirements for a different sized quilt will be given — elsewhere you will have to estimate it. If you require your quilt to be a specific size, compare this with the measurements of the example quilt before you start, and adapt the instructions accordingly.

All the quilt tops in this book are designed to be completed over a fairly intensive two- or three-day sewing 'binge'! The quickest (Single and Double Irish Chains and Lone Star) can be completed by a fairly efficient sewer in less than 10 hours. The Basket Quilt probably takes the longest — perhaps 25 hours for a 30-block Queen sized quilt.

Read through the entire chapter before beginning any of the quilts, so that you have an overview of the instructions. This will save some time when you are sewing — as you will have some idea of what's coming next.

There is only one rule in patchwork, whether it is by traditional or modern methods, and that is *be accurate* — in folding, measuring, cutting and sewing — and it will all fit together like a jigsaw. Patchwork really *is* painless!

Conversion of
Imperial measurements
used in this book

¼″	6 mm
½″	1.25 cm
¾″	2 cm
1″	2.5 cm
1¼″	3 cm
1½″	3.75 cm
1¾″	4.5 cm
2″	5 cm
2¼″	5.75 cm
2½″	6.25 cm
2¾″	7 cm
3″	7.7 cm
5¼″	13.5 cm
5½″	14 cm
6¼″	16 cm
6½″	16.5 cm
10½″	26.5 cm
14½″	36.75 cm

CHAPTER 1

IRISH CHAINS
SINGLE, DOUBLE AND TRIPLE

THE SINGLE IRISH CHAIN

The quilt patterns in Chapters 1-3 of this book are all variations on Seminole piecing (see Introduction). Probably the simplest manifestation of the Seminole technique as a block is the Nine-patch block. This block is the basis of the Single Irish Chain.

If you have never done any strip piecing or experimented with a rotary cutter before, this is a good place to start!

The Single Irish Chain instructions set out here are for a cot quilt. However, you may like to start by making a couple of double Nine-patch (also called *Nine-patch of nine-patches)* cushions. (Figure 1.1)

Instructions for finishing the cushion can be found in the chapter on the Trip Around the World method (Chapter 2).

A Nine-patch block also makes an excellent Noughts and Crosses board that can be used on car strips, etc. (This wonderful idea is from Judy Turner.) Make up a Nine-patch block using three inch strips of fabric. Machine quilt it using machine weight (¼ inch/6 mm) batting and stitching along the seam lines. Bind the edges and add a pocket to the back to hold the noughts and crosses, which should be cut from felt. (Figure 1.2)

Figure 1.1

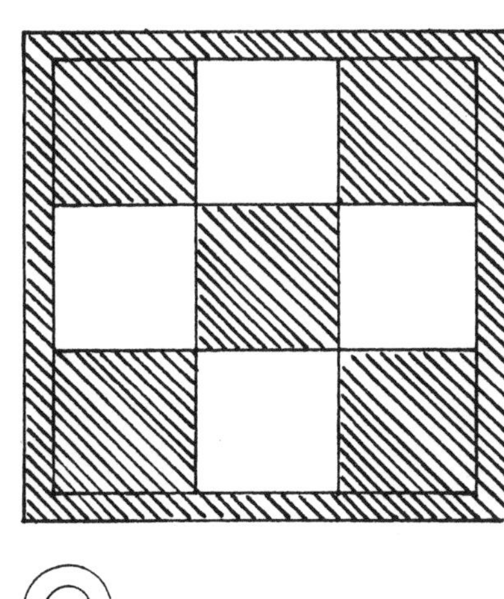

Figure 1.2

PIECING THE NINE-PATCH BLOCKS

Using two contrasting fabrics and the rotary cutter cut 2½ inch strips across the full width of the fabric, following the instructions for cutting and piecing in the Introduction.

Join batches of strips together as indicated below, using ¼ inch/6 mm seam allowance. Press all seam allowances in the one direction. (Figure 1.3)

Figure 1.3

Re-cut units vertically in 2½ inch strips. You will need twice as many strips from Unit 1 as you will from Unit 2. (Figure 1.4)

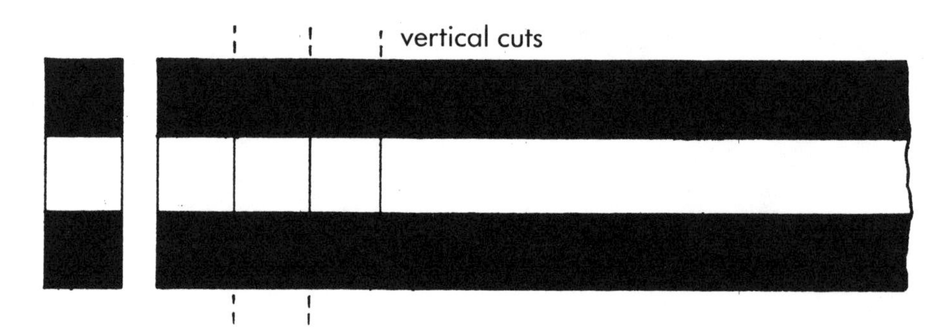

Figure 1.4

Join together strips of alternating units to form Nine-patch blocks, turning each strip so that adjoining seam allowances face in opposite directions (see Introduction notes on Butted Seams). (Figure 1.5)

These Nine-patch blocks form the basis of the Single Irish Chain quilt, but also make wonderful scrap quilts, using a wide variety of fabrics divided into general light and dark groupings.

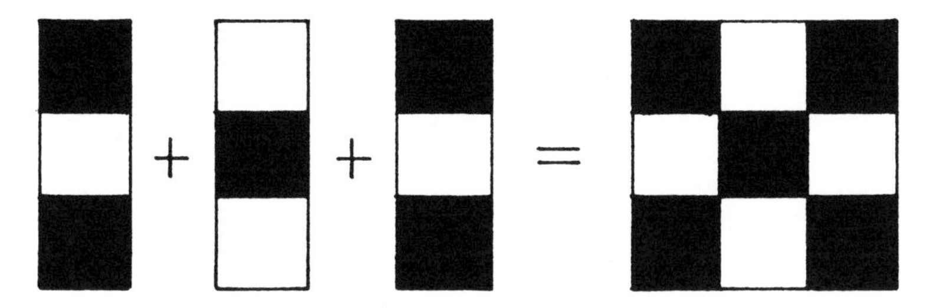

Figure 1.5

THE SINGLE IRISH CHAIN COT QUILT

The Single Irish Chain pattern is made up of Nine-patch blocks alternated with plain (unpieced) blocks. The following instructions are for a quilt measuring approximately 95 cm x 125 cm (38 inches x 49 inches).

Two fabrics are used:

- Fabric 1 (□) is used in the Nine-patch blocks and for the unpieced squares in between.
- Fabric 2 (■) is used only in the Nine-patch blocks.

Figure 1.6 Single Irish Chain Cot Quilt

REQUIREMENTS

Fabric 1 — 1.2 m (1⅜ yds)
for the blocks, plus another 1.1 m (1¼ yds) if you wish to use Fabric 1 for the border

Fabric 2 — 80 cm (⅞ yd)

You may wish to introduce another fabric for the border, or have a series of borders.
Fabric requirements for alternative borders will have to be estimated separately.

METHOD

Step 1 — Using the rotary cutter, cut horizontal strips across the full width of the fabric as follows, following the instructions for cutting and piecing in the introduction.

Fabric 1 — Seven 2½ inch strips
Three 6½ inch strips
Fabric 2 — Eight 2½ inch strips

Step 2 — Join batches of the 2½ inch strips into Units 1 and 2 of the Nine-patch piecing as described on page 12.

You will need to make up three of Unit 1 and two of Unit 2.

Figure 1.7

Unit 1

Figure 1.8

Unit 2

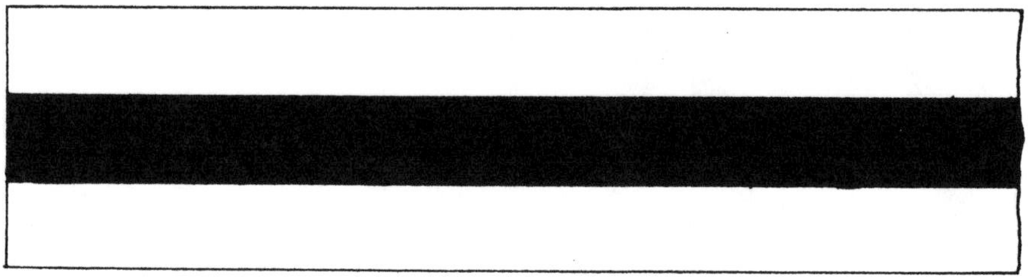

Step 3 — From these make up eighteen Nine-patch blocks as described on page 13.

Step 4 — Now cut the 6½ inch strips of Fabric 1 vertically to form 6½ inch squares.

You will need seventeen squares. (Figure 1.9)

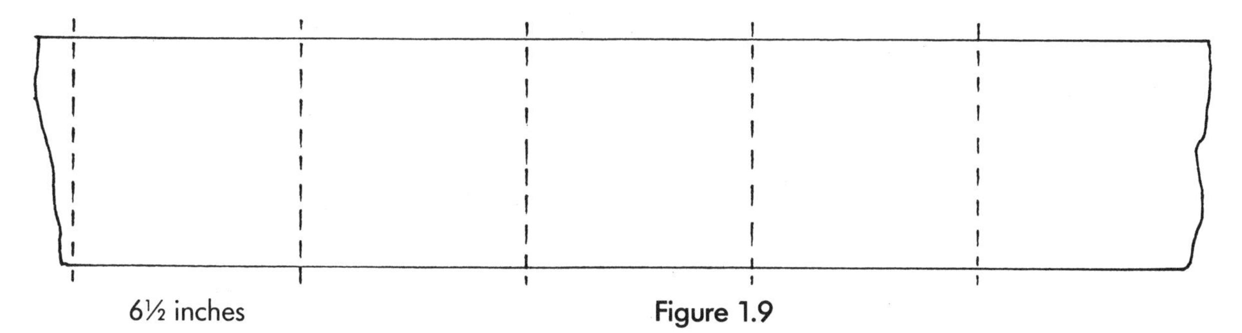

Figure 1.9

Step 5 — Join together five blocks at a time to form rows of the quilt, alternating between Nine-patch blocks and unpieced squares. Begin the first row with a Nine-patch block, the second with a plain block, and so on. You will need to make 4 rows beginning with a Nine-patch block and 3 rows beginning with a plain block to make 7 rows all together. (Figure 1.10)

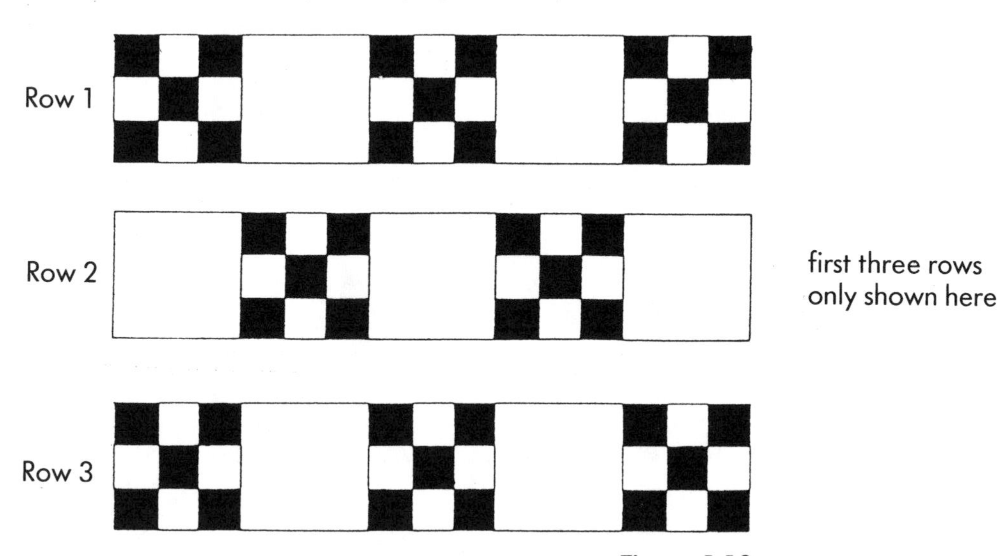

first three rows only shown here

Figure 1.10

Step 6 — Press all the seam allowances between the blocks towards the unpieced blocks. Join the rows of blocks so that the seam allowances butt together neatly (see Introduction).

Your quilt is now ready for the border — see Chapter 6.

Figure 1.11 Double Irish Chain Quilt

THE DOUBLE IRISH CHAIN QUILT

The Double Irish Chain design, like the Single Irish Chain, consists of two different blocks which alternate across the quilt to form the pattern. The techniques employed are the same as those used for the Single Chain, but with a larger number of strips to create a more complex pattern.

The following instructions are for a quilt measuring approximately 175 cm x 225 cm (68 inches x 88 inches). Borders measure 25 cm (10 inches).

Three fabrics are used:

- Fabric 1 (□) — forms the plain (unpieced) centres of block 1 and may also be used for the borders.
- Fabric 2 (▩) — forms the outside edges of the 'chain'.
- Fabric 3 (■) — forms the inside of the 'chain'.

Figure 1.12 Block 1 Block 2

REQUIREMENTS

Fabric 1 — 4.2 m (4⅝ yds).
(This includes 2.3 m (2½ yds) for the border.
A different fabric may be used if desired)

Fabric 2 — 1.4 m (1⅝ yds)

Fabric 3 — 80 cm (⅞ yd)

METHOD

Step 1 — Using the rotary cutter, cut horizontal strips across the full width of the fabric as follows, following the instructions for cutting and piecing in the Introduction.

Fabric 1 — Three 6½ inch strips
Three 10½ inch strips
Five 2½ inch strips
Fabric 2 — Nineteen 2½ inch strips
Fabric 3 — Eleven 2½ inch strips

Step 2 — Join together batches of strips as indicated below, using a ¼ inch/6 mm seam allowance. You will notice that there are seven units to be pieced using full widths of fabric, and another four which use only a quarter of a strip. The reason for this is simple. You will need a little more than the one or two full-width units to make up the blocks, but to piece an extra full width of each unit would be wasteful of both time and fabric when only a small part of it is needed — hence the quarters. Piece all the full width units first, then cut the remaining strips of fabric into four and piece the quarter units.

Unit 1A — use 6½ inch strips of Fabric 1 and 2½ inch strips of Fabric 2

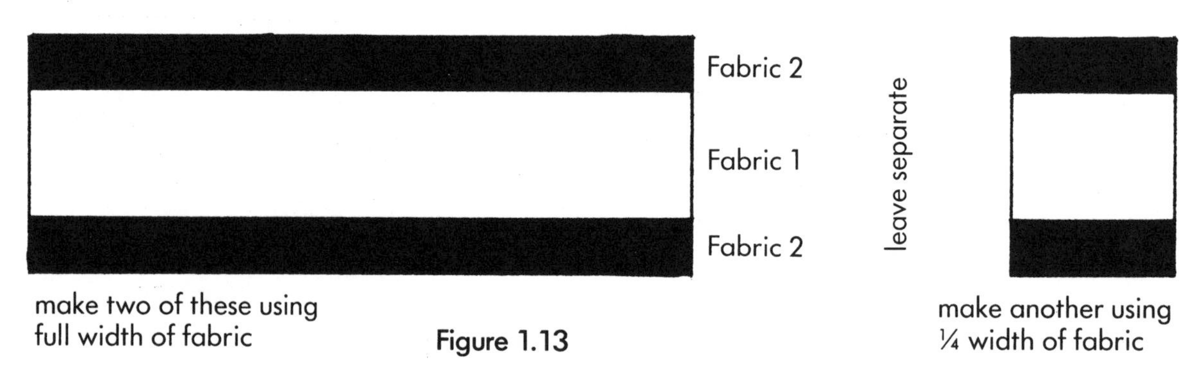

Figure 1.13

Unit 1B — this consists of the three 10½ inch strips of Fabric 1. No piecing of these is required at present.

Units 1A and 1B will be used to make Block 1

Unit 2A — use 2½ inch strips of Fabrics 1, 2 and 3

Figure 1.14

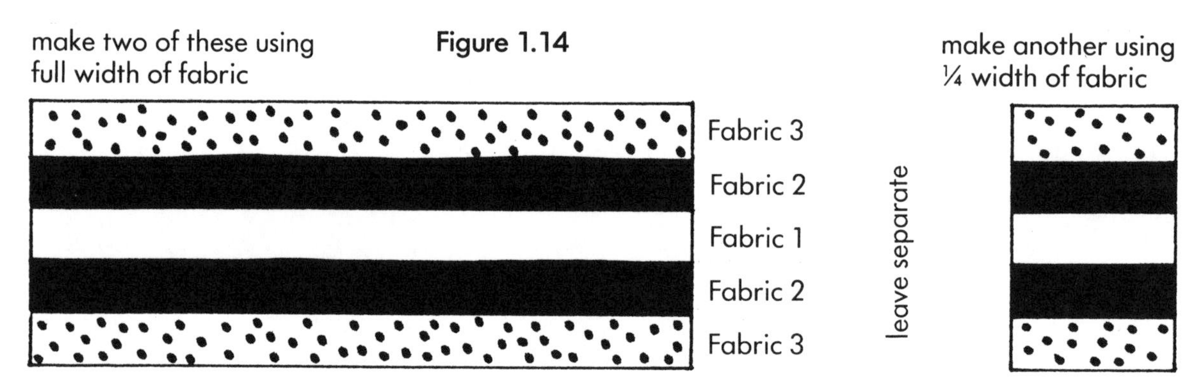

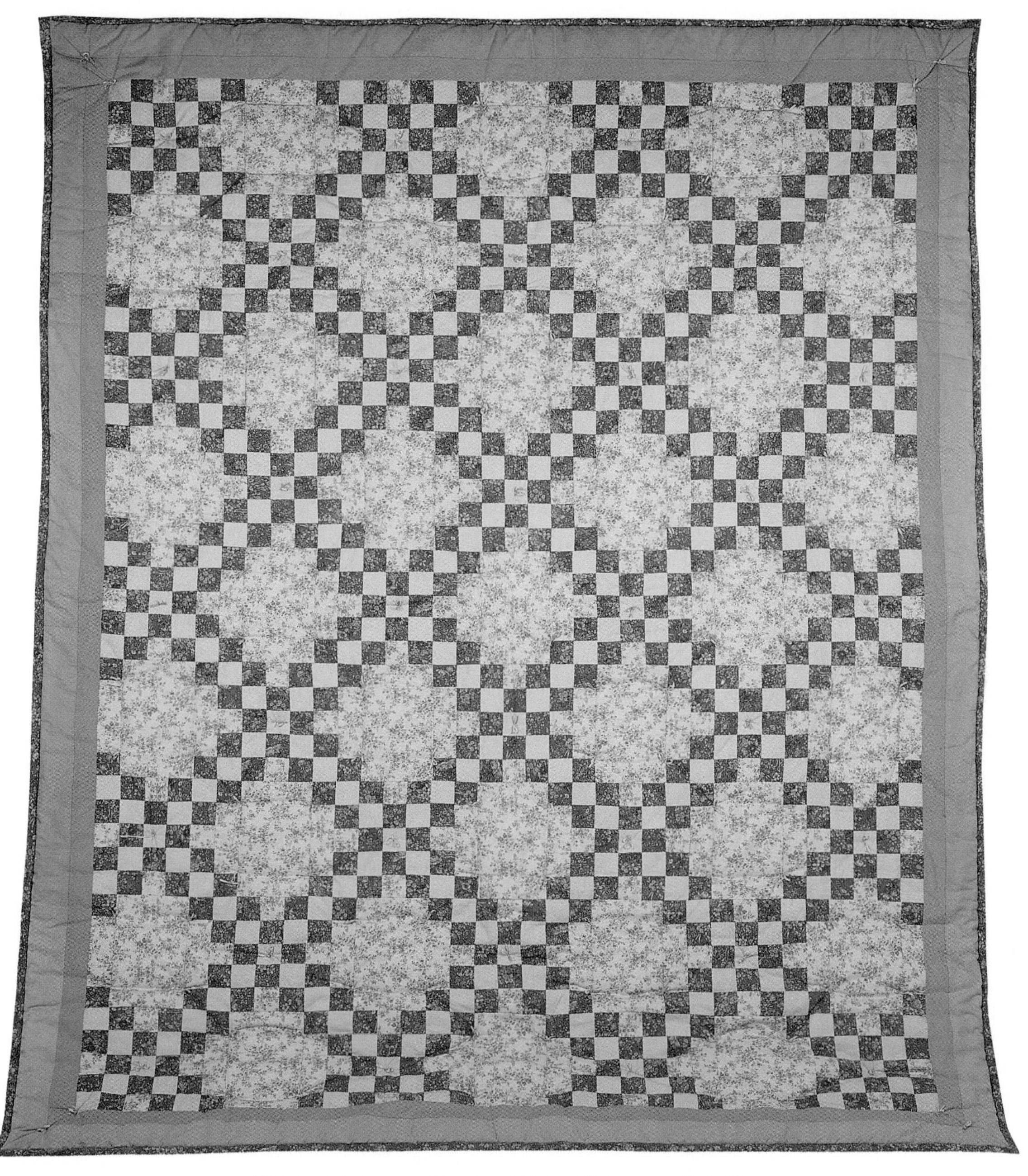

Queen bed-sized Double Irish Chain by Sue Gill
consisting of 63 blocks. Sue's husband David helped her to
tie the 155 satin bows which hold the quilt together.

DOUBLE IRISH CHAIN BY ROSEMARY DONOUGHUE
Hand-quilted with traditional Amish wreaths and triple ropes.

DOUBLE IRISH CHAIN BY AILSA MILLS
Tie-quilted. The plain chain appears to 'float' over the printed background.

MINIATURE DOUBLE IRISH CHAIN BY ANNE WHITSED
measuring only 16 cm x 20 cm. It was pieced using strip-piecing methods.

Trip Around the World Quilt by Carmel Ellis
Tie-quilted.

Trip Around the World Quilt by Ailsa Mills
Tie-quilted.

SUNSHINE AND SHADOW QUILT BY SUE GILL
Sue worked out the strip-piecing necessary to make this variation on Trip Around the World, and tie-quilted it with pink and green pearl crochet cotton.

Log Cabin Quilt in Barn Raising setting by Pam Hendy
features a strong light/dark contrast and striking red centres.
Tie-quilted with satin ribbon.

Log Cabin Quilt by Denise Nielsen
makes another striking light/dark contrast. The setting is Straight Furrows.
Blocks are tie-quilted, with hand-quilting in the borders.

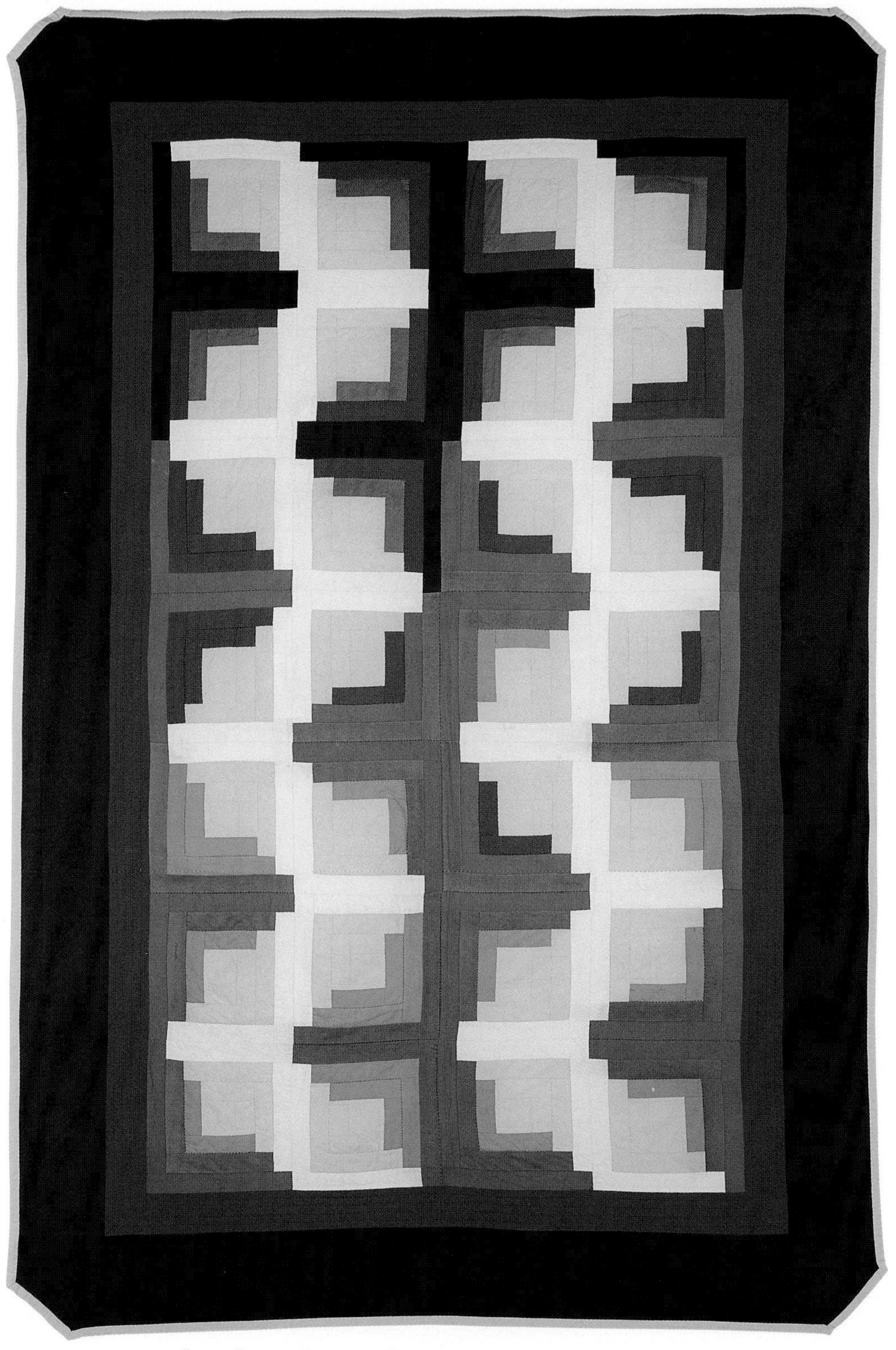

Log Cabin Quilt in Streak of Lightning setting by
Maryann Rowland
is shaded to represent lightning in a night sky. Hand-quilted.

LOG CABIN QUILT BY ROBYN PARRY

A wide variety of fabrics were used to make this quilt with a sea scene. The sails of the boats were hand-appliquéd on. Hand-quilted with nautical motifs by Sally Mansfield.

LONE STAR QUILT BY ROBYN PARRY
This quilt has an extra pocket on the back to hold a doona. Hand-quilted by Sally Mansfield with designs taken from the paisley fabric.

LONE STAR SET ON POINT BY ROS MILLER
Beautifully hand-quilted, with an effective use of strip-piecing in the binding.

Lone Star Quilt by Sharon Pick
The chintz background is heavily hand-quilted in traditional Amish designs.

Lone Star Quilt by Alyson Crawford
Heavily hand-quilted with radiating lines, feather wreaths, cross hatching and an alligator.

LONE STAR QUILT BY GAL MCLELLAN
In this striking quilt the background print picks up the colours of the star. Note the clever use of strip-piecing offcuts in the border and binding.
Hand-quilted by Fran Armstrong.

BASKET QUILT BY ROBYN PARRY

Hand-quilted by Desley Drevins. A fine, contrasting border sets off the basket blocks from the background.

AMISH BASKET DOONA COVER BY ANNE WHITSED
Unquilted.

BASKET QUILT BY ROSEMARY DONOUGHUE
Traditional Amish colours. To be hand-quilted.

AMISH BASKET QUILT BY ROSEMARY DONOUGHUE
Hand-quilted.

TRIP AROUND THE WORLD CUSHION BY ROSEMARY DONOUGHUE
Unquilted.

COT QUILT FOR JACKSON TURNER BY ROSEMARY DONOUGHUE
The reduction of scale from 2″ squares to 1″ squares brings this 35-block Double Irish Chain quilt down to cot size.
Hand-quilted.

Lone Star Quilt by Susan Manderson
This close-up shows the layers basted together ready for hand-quilting.

Unit 2B — use 2½ inch strips of Fabrics 2 and 3

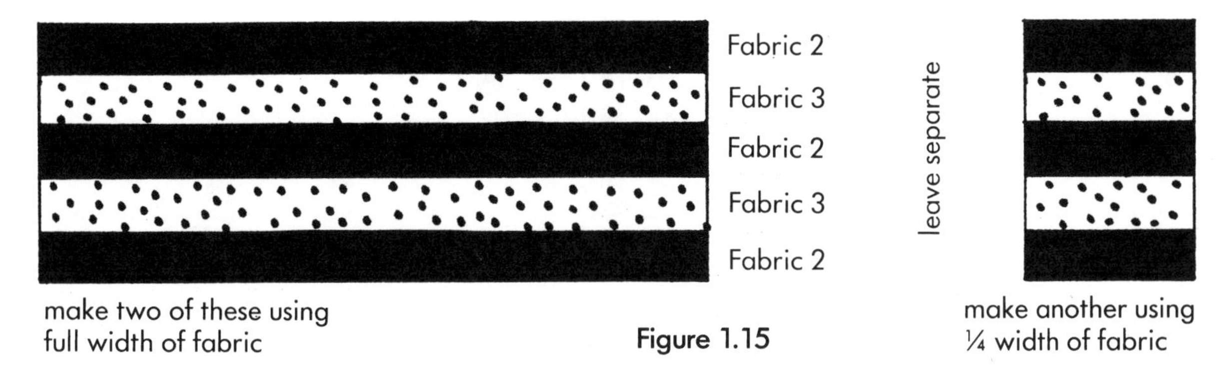

Figure 1.15

Unit 2C — use 2½ inch strips of Fabrics 1, 2 and 3

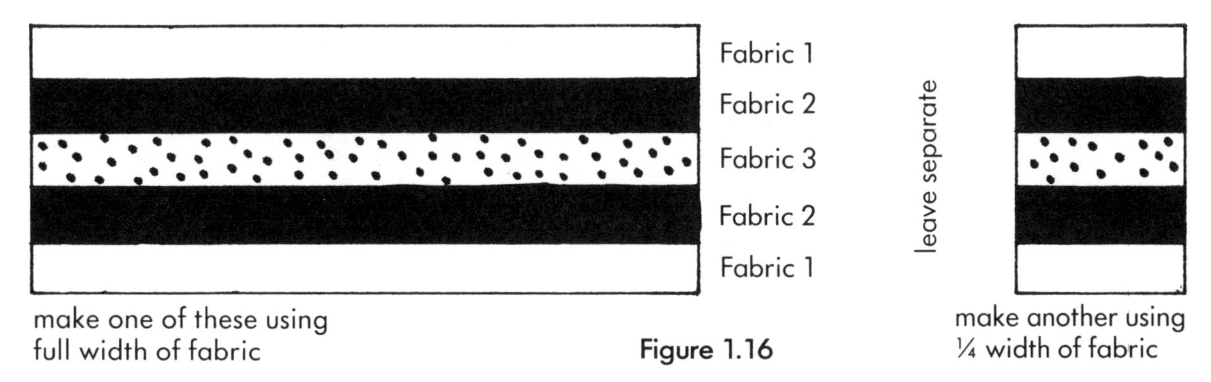

Figure 1.16

Units 2A, 2B and 2C will be used to make Block 2. Iron all seam allowances in the one direction on each unit.

Step 3 — Re-cut units 1A, 2A, 2B and 2C vertically into 2½ inch strips, having first trimmed the left-hand side so that it is perpendicular to the seam lines. You may find you have to re-trim this edge several times while cutting vertical strips, as the units can become slightly distorted from sewing. Check the vertical edge after every four or five cuts. (Figure 1.17)

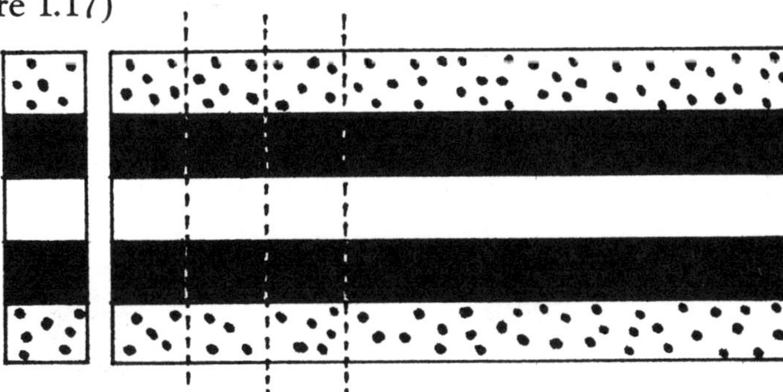

Figure 1.17

A full width of fabric should yield 15-16 vertical strips. You will need:

34 strips of Unit 1A
36 strips of Unit 2A
36 strips of Unit 2B
18 strips of Unit 2C

Now re-cut the only remaining unit, 1B (the 10½ inch strips of fabric), vertically into 6½ inch strips. You will need 17 of these. (Figure 1.18)

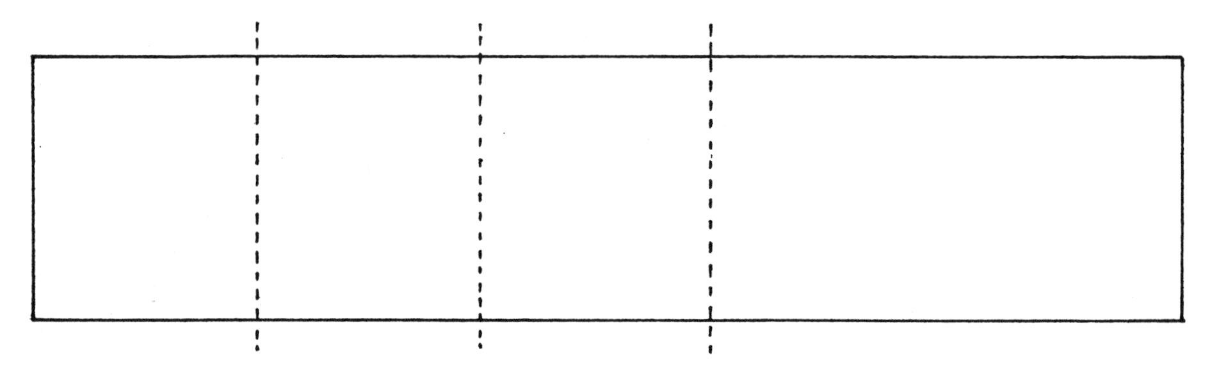

Figure 1.18

Step 4 — Join together strips from Units 1A and 1B to form Block 1. Make sure the seam allowances on both the side strips face the same way. (Figure 1.19)

Make 17 of Block 1

Figure 1.19

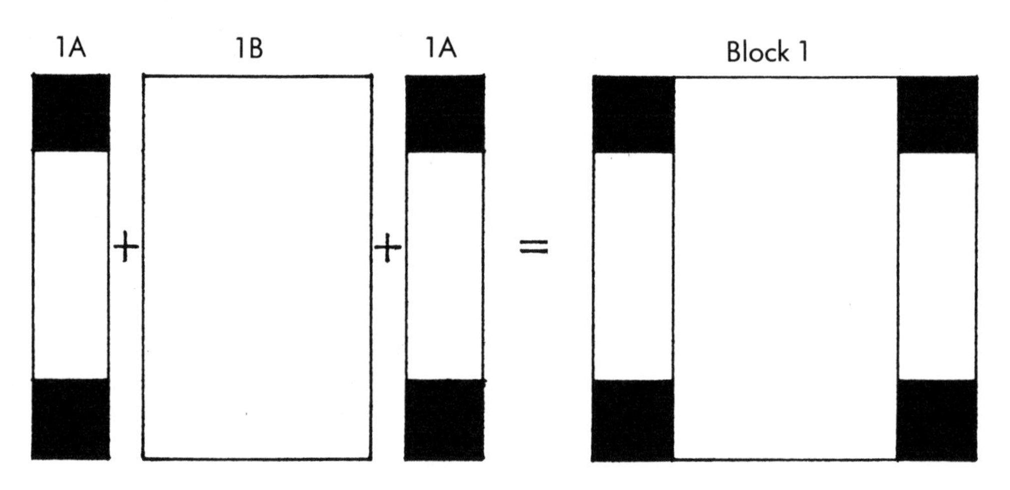

Join together strips from Units 2A, 2B and 2C to form Block 2. It will help if you turn each strip so that its seam allowance faces the opposite direction to the one next to it (see Introduction for notes on butting seams together). (Figure 1.20)

Make 18 of Block 2

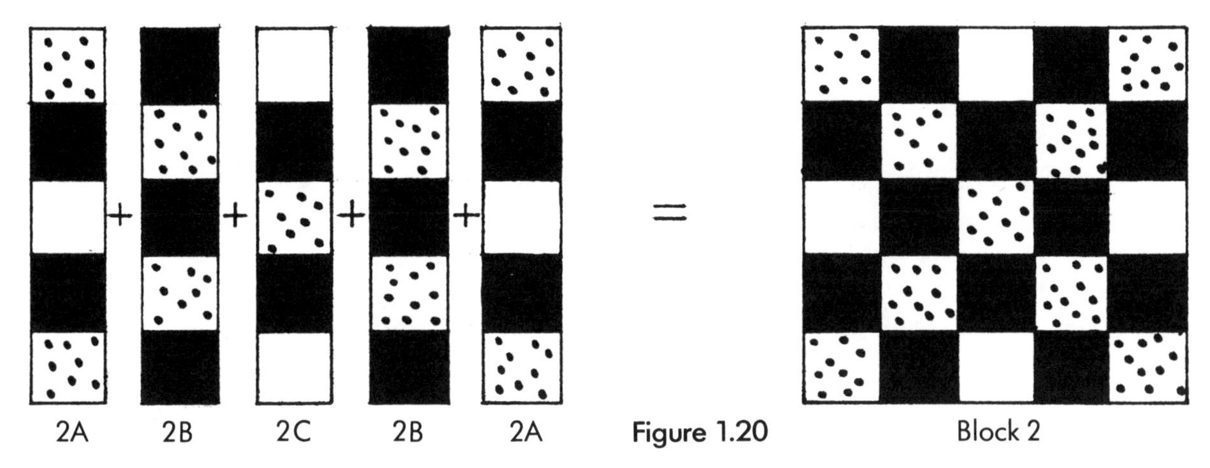

Figure 1.20

Step 5 — Beginning with Block 2, join together five alternating blocks in a row to form the first row of the quilt. Join another five blocks for the second row, this time beginning with Block 1. The third row will begin with Block 2, and so on. Continue this way until you have seven rows. Try to make sure that the blocks are placed in such a way that the vertical seam allowances can still be ironed in either direction before the rows of blocks are joined.

Step 6 — Now join the seven rows together, ensuring that Block 2 is at the four corners of the quilt. Remember again that ironing seam allowances in the opposite direction on each row will reduce bulk and create neater intersections. (Figure 1.21)

You are now ready to add the border — see Chapter 6.

Figure 1.21

Block 2	Block 1	Block 2	Block 1	Block 2
Block 1	Block 2	Block 1	Block 2	Block 1

continue for seven rows

Figure 1.22

Triple Irish Chain Quilt

THE TRIPLE IRISH CHAIN QUILT

The principle behind the piecing of the Triple Irish Chain blocks is identical to that of the Double Irish Chain but the blocks will be bigger. While the Double Chain uses three fabrics, the Triple Chain uses four fabrics, and the finished blocks will measure 14 inches/35 cm, as opposed to the Double Irish Chain's 10 inch/25 cm blocks.

Thus a Triple Irish Chain quilt with the same configuration of thirty-five blocks (five across, seven down) with a 25 cm (10 inch) border will measure 225 cm x 295 cm (88 inches x 117 inches). This makes it ideal for a Queen or King sized bed.

The four fabrics used are:

- Fabric 1 (□) — this forms the plain (unpieced) centres of Block 1.
- Fabric 2 (▨) and Fabric 3 — (⚄) — these form the outer edges of the chain.
- Fabric 4 (■) this forms the inside of the chain.

REQUIREMENTS

For the blocks you will need:

Fabric 1 — 3 m (3⅜ yds); Fabric 3 — 2.2 m (2½ yds);
Fabric 2 — 1.9 m (2⅛ yds); Fabric 4 — 1.3 m (1½ yds)

In addition you will require fabric for the border.
For a single border you will need:
2.6 m (2⅞ yds) for straight cut border
or 3.1 m (3½ yds) for mitred borders,
or you may wish to add multiple borders.
See Chapter 6 for more information.

METHOD

Step 1 — Using the rotary cutter, cut horizontal strips across the full width of the fabric as follows, following the instructions for cutting and piecing in the Introduction.

Fabric 1 — five 2½ inch strips
three 6½ inch strips
three 10½ inch strips
three 14½ inch strips

Fabric 2 — twenty-three 2½ inch strips

Fabric 3 — twenty-seven 2½ inch strips

Fabric 4 — fifteen 2½ inch strips

Step 2 — Join together batches of strips as indicated below, using a ¼ inch/6 mm seam allowance.

You will notice that there are 11 units to be pieced using full widths of fabric, and another five using only a quarter width. The reason for this is simple. You will need a little more than the one or two full width units to make up the blocks, but to piece an extra full width of each unit would be wasteful of both time and fabric when only a small part of it is needed. Hence the quarters. Piece all the full widths first, then cut the remaining strips of fabric into four and piece the quarter units.

Unit 1A — use 2½ inch strips of Fabrics 2 and 3 and 6½ inch strips of Fabric 1.

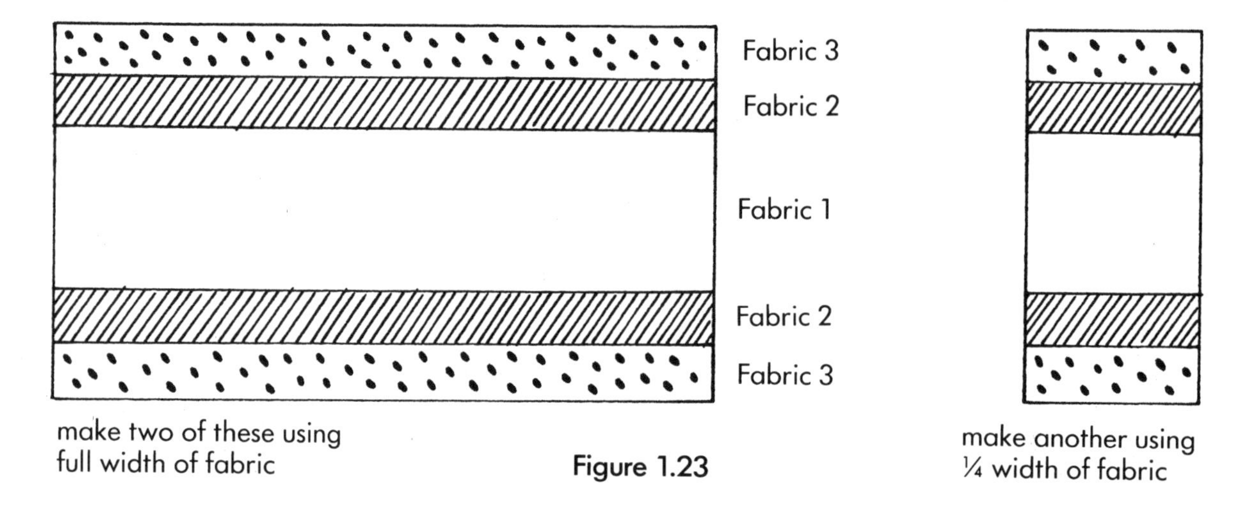

Figure 1.23

Unit 1B — use 2½ inch strips of Fabric 2 and 10½ inch strips of Fabric 1.

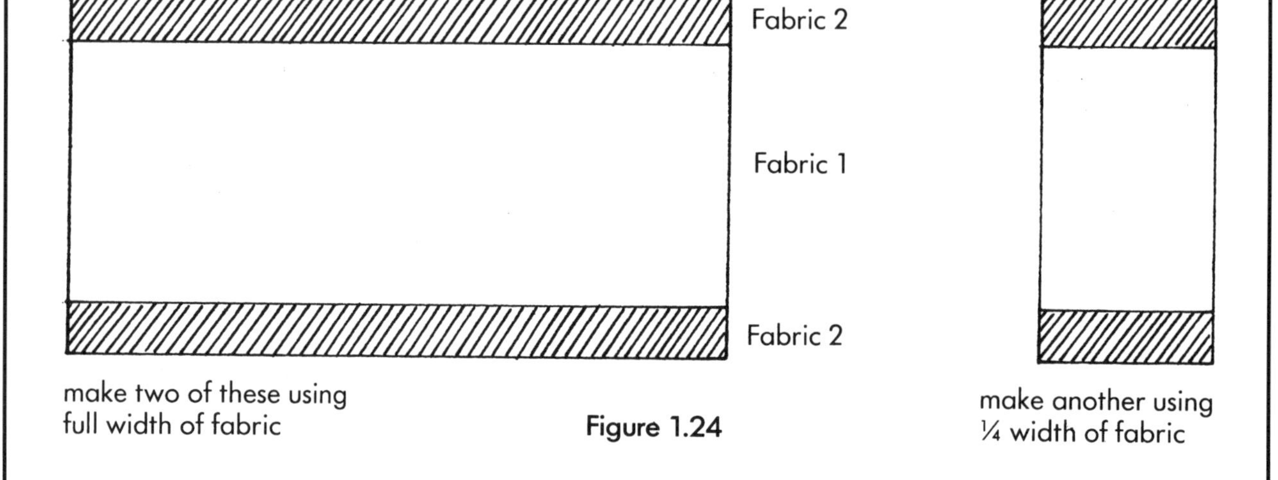

Figure 1.24

Unit 1C — this consists of the three separate 14½ inch strips of Fabric 1. No piecing is required at present.

Units 1A, 1B and 1C will be used to make Block 1.

Unit 2A — use 2½ inch strips of Fabrics 1, 2, 3 and 4

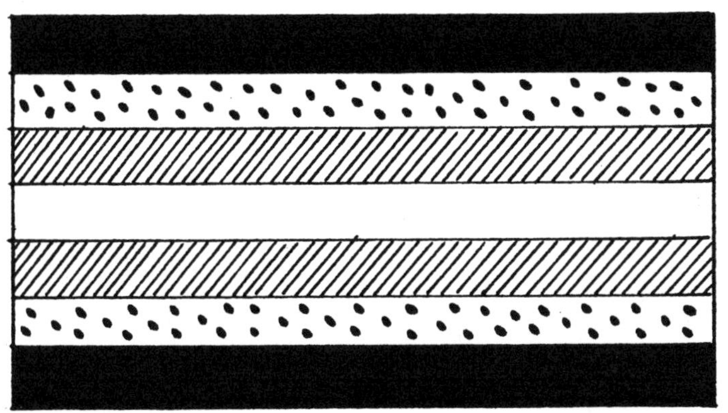

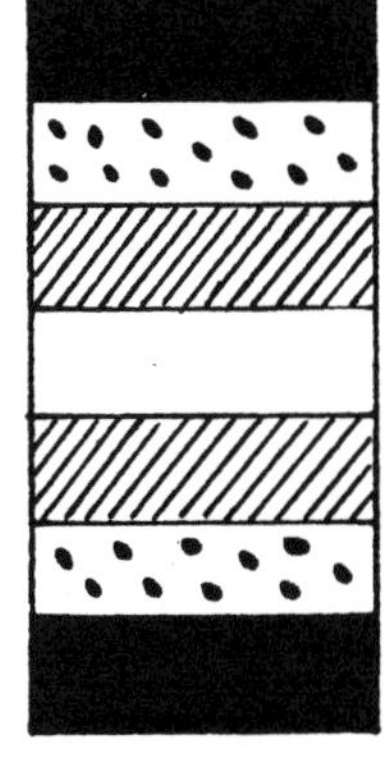

make two of these using full width of fabric

make another using ¼ width of fabric

Figure 1.25

Unit 2B — use 2½ inch strips of Fabrics 2, 3 and 4

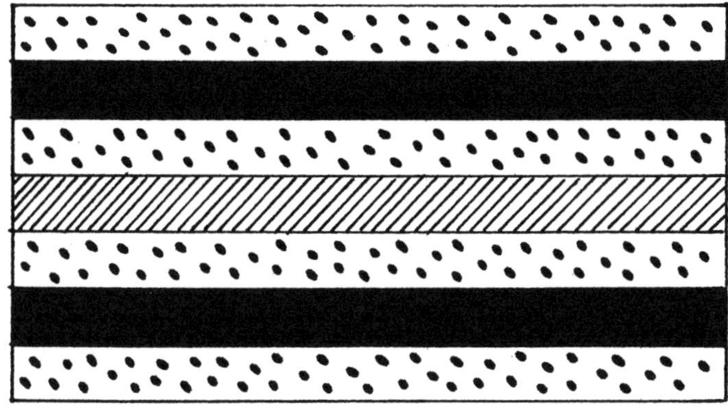

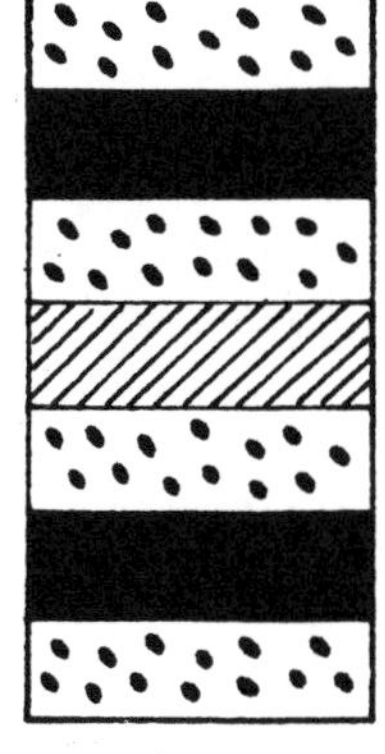

make two of these using full width of fabric

make another using ¼ width of fabric

Figure 1.26

Unit 2C — use 2½ inch strips of Fabrics 2, 3 and 4

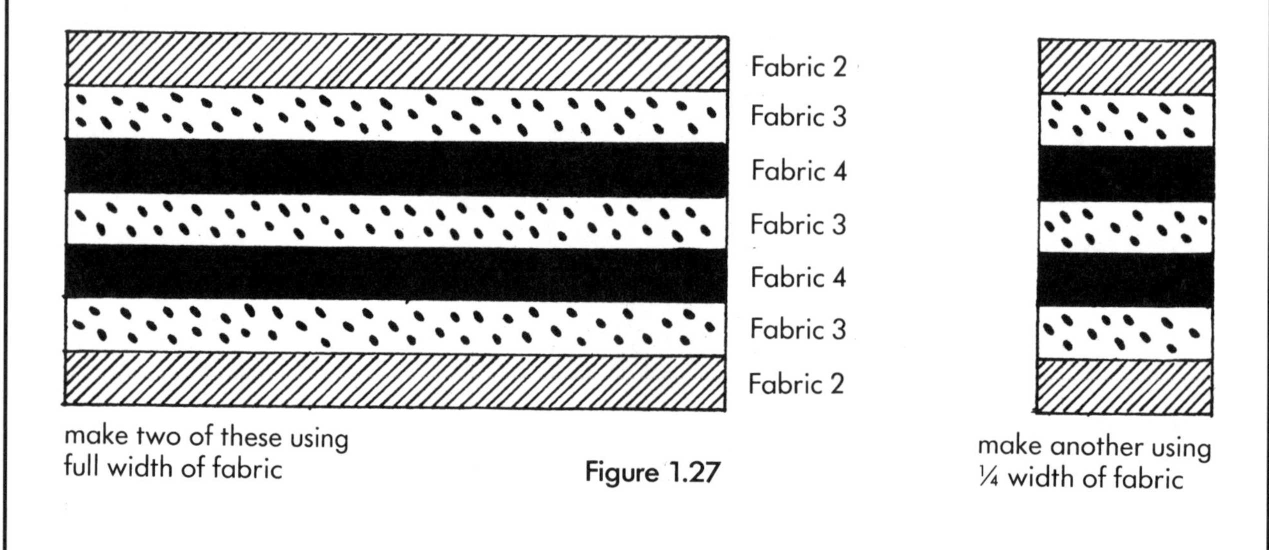

Figure 1.27

Unit 2D — use 2½ inch strips of Fabrics 1, 2, 3 and 4

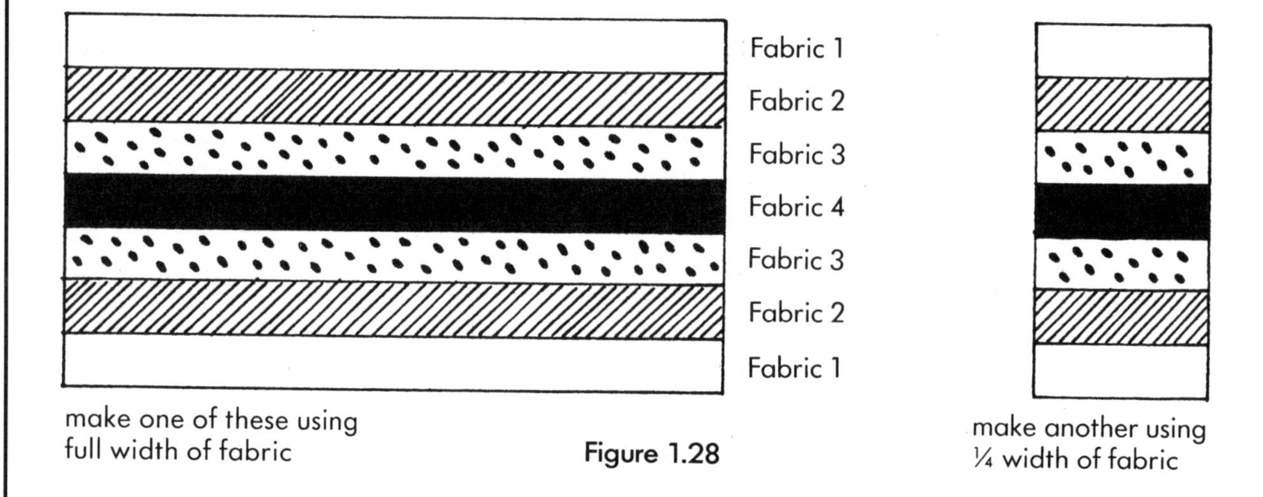

Figure 1.28

Units 2A, 2B, 2C and 2D will be used together to make Block 2. Iron all seam allowances in one direction on each unit.

Step 3 — Now re-cut Unit 1C (the 14½ inch strips of Fabric 1) vertically into 6½ inch strips. You will need 17 of these vertical strips.

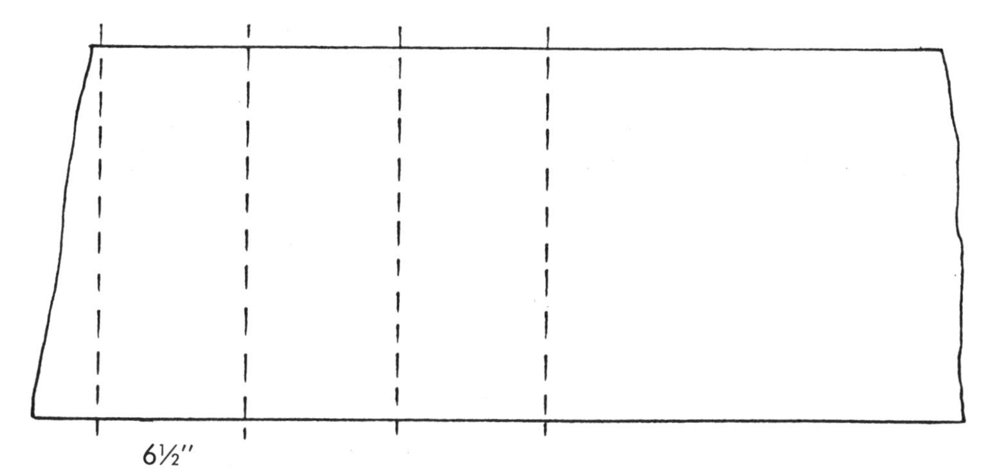

Figure 1.29

Re-cut Units 1A, 1B, 2A, 2B, 2C and 2D vertically into 2½ inch strips, having first straightened the left-hand side so that it is perpendicular to the seam lines. Because the units may be slightly distorted from sewing you will have to re-check the perpendicular edge after every 5-6 cuts. (Figure 1.30)

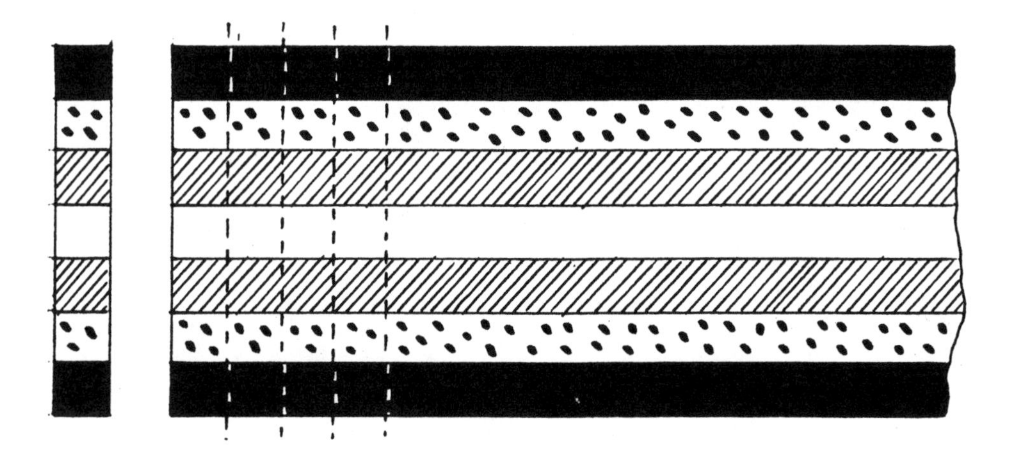

Figure 1.30

You will require:
- 34 strips of Units 1A and 1B
- 36 strips of Units 2A, 2B and 2C
- 18 strips of Unit 2D

A full width of fabric should yield 15-16 strips.

Step 4 — Join together strips from Units 1A, 1B and 1C to form Block 1. Make sure seam allowances on the outside edges are both facing the same way. (Figure 1.31)
Make 17 of Block 1

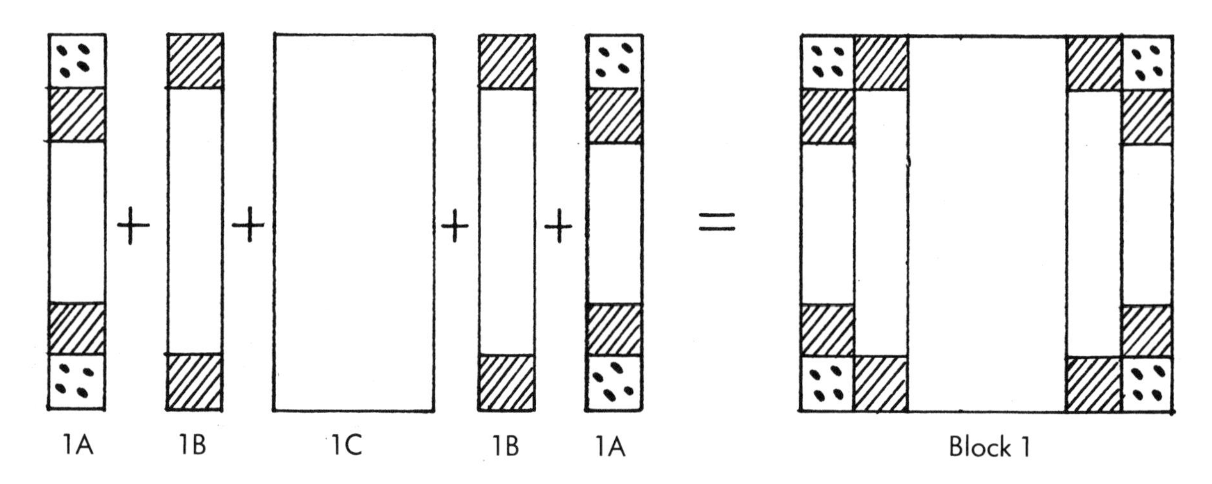

Figure 1.31

Join together strips from Units 2A, 2B, 2C and 2D to form Block 2. It will help if you butt together seam allowances (see Introduction). (Figure 1.32)
Make 18 of Block 2

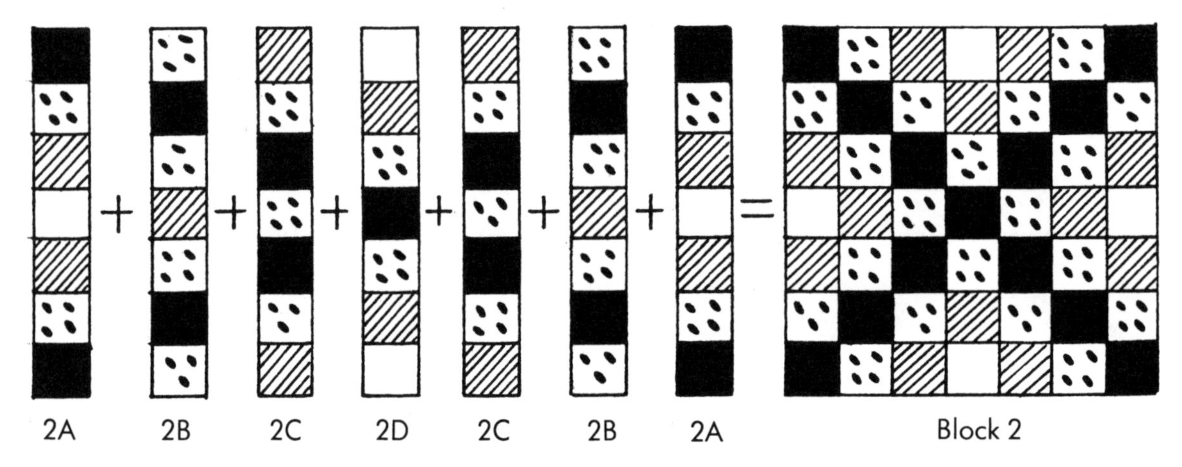

Figure 1.32

Step 5 — Beginning with Block 2, join together five alternating blocks in a row to form the first row of the quilt. Join another five blocks to form the second row, this time beginning with Block 1. Continue like this until you have seven rows. Make sure the blocks are placed so that the vertical seam allowances can be ironed in either direction.

Press each row of blocks so that all the seam allowances face one way, then join the seven rows together, butting together the seams. There should be a Block 2 in each corner of the quilt. (Figure 1.33)

Your quilt is now ready for its border — refer to Chapter 6.

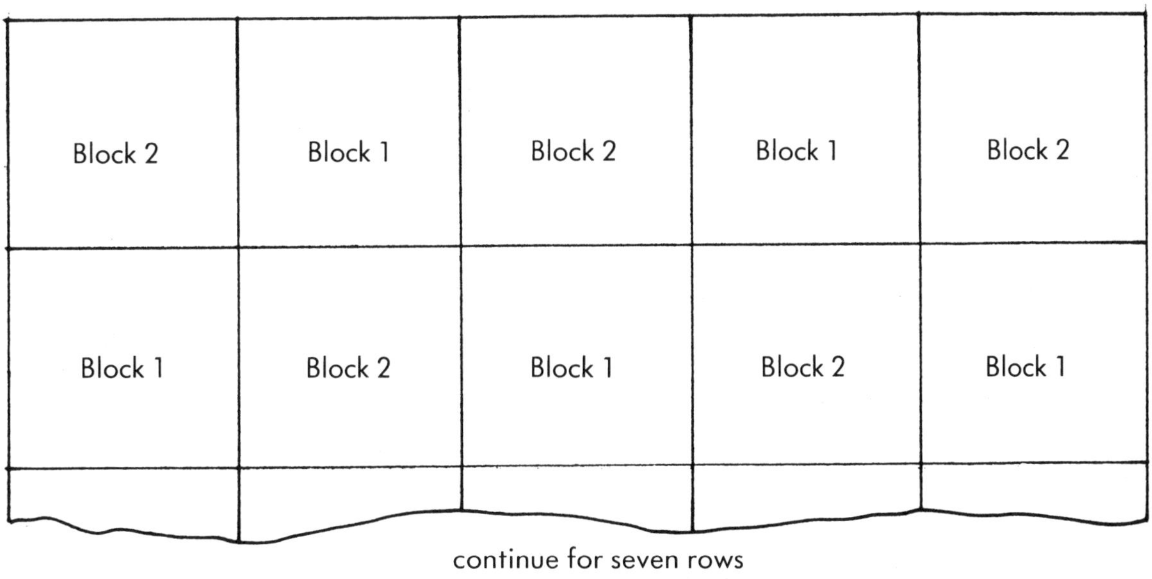

Block 2	Block 1	Block 2	Block 1	Block 2
Block 1	Block 2	Block 1	Block 2	Block 1

continue for seven rows

Figure 1.33

HOW TO ALTER THE SIZE OF THE IRISH CHAIN QUILTS

Because the Irish Chain quilts are all made from a pair of alternating blocks, it is impossible to increase the quilt size by one block all round — this would unbalance the pattern. Any increase in the number of blocks must be a multiple of two blocks in either direction.

Thus the next size up from the example Double Irish Chain (5 blocks x 7 rows = 35 blocks) would be seven blocks by nine rows, or 63 blocks — a considerable increase in piecing! It should be noted that the dimensions of a 63-block Double Irish Chain are similar to those of a 35-block Triple Irish Chain.

Another possibility is to alter the size of the strip piecing. The Double Irish Chain cot quilt in plate 21 is a 35-block quilt using 1½ inch, 3½ inch and 5½ inch strips.

The use of multiple borders, perhaps incorporating some additional piecing, will add considerable size to a quilt — see Chapter 6.

CHAPTER 2

TRIP AROUND THE WORLD

The 'Trip Around the World' is sometimes also called 'Sunshine and Shadow', although the classic Amish Sunshine and Shadow quilts were an arrangement of squares which formed diamond-shaped bands of colour, rather than diamonds which form concentric squares of colour. (Figure 2.1)

The Amish quilts were generally square, which presented no problem in piecing either of these variations, but quilts today are more often rectangular, and the Trip Around the World variation lends itself more readily to being extended into a rectangle.

Figure 2.1

Classic Sunshine and Shadow

Sunshine and Shadow variation
(also called Trip Around the World)

This chapter begins with instructions for a cushion cover, which demonstrates the Trip Around the World method made into a square. The quilt instructions which follow it will demonstrate how the square can be extended into a rectangle.

The piecing of this quilt leaves little room for effective hand-quilting, making tie-quilting a reasonable alternative. The instructions here are for a single bed sized quilt, and combined with tie-quilting this would make an ideal child's quilt.

The 'Trip Around the World' method can be readily adapted to make gifts that look like they've taken months to make — a great way to satisfy those friends and relatives who hear you've taken up patchwork and ask 'will you make me a quilt?'

TRIP AROUND THE WORLD CUSHION

The following instructions are for a cushion measuring approximately 45 cm (18 inches) square.

Four fabrics are used in a repeat sequence. (Figure 2.2)

REQUIREMENTS

25 cm (¼ yd) each of four fabrics, to be known here as Fabrics A, B, C and D.
An additional 1 metre (1⅛ yds) of one of the fabrics will be required for the cushion ruffle and back.
The use of Fabric A for the ruffle will make for a smoother flow between the half-squares, on the edge of the cushion, and the ruffle, but this is not mandatory.
(Figure 2.2)

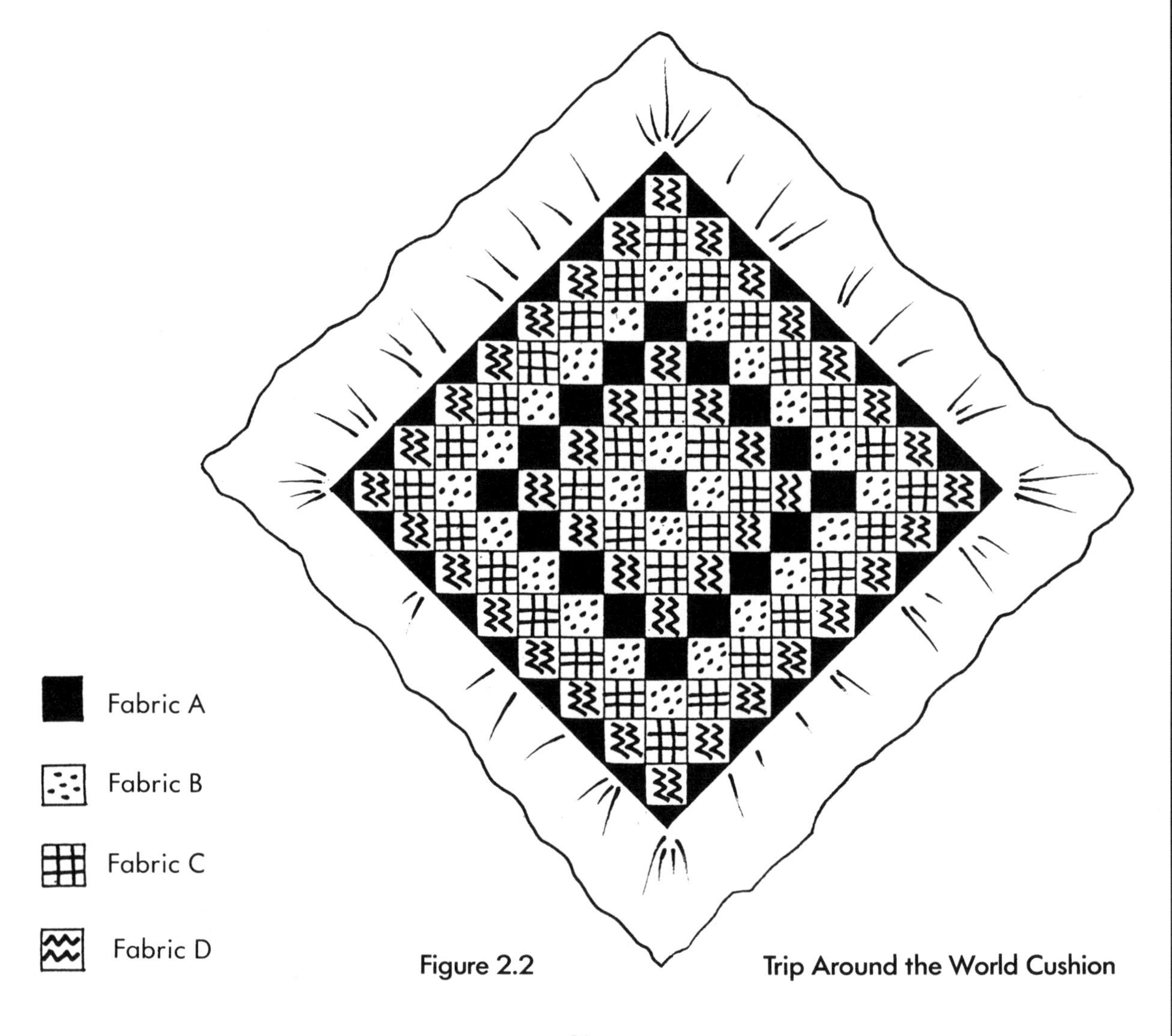

Figure 2.2 Trip Around the World Cushion

METHOD

Step 1 — Using four different fabrics, A, B, C and D, and the rotary cutter, cut 2 inch horizontal strips across the full width of the fabric as follows, following the instructions for cutting and piecing in the introduction.

You will need:
3 strips Fabric A (if using 90 cm (36 inch) fabric cut 4 strips of A)
2 strips Fabric B
2 strips Fabric C
2 strips Fabric D

The fabric sequence runs from the centre of the cushion outwards – Fabric A is at the centre and is repeated on the outside edge.

Step 2 — Cut to size and join fabric strips as indicated below, aligning fabrics on the left-hand edge, to form a 'stepped' unit of strips. Note that from Row 7 onwards you will have to join additional strips separately, as the width of the fabric will not make a long enough 'step'. There is no need to join this second group of strips to the first. (Figure 2.3)

Rows 6-9 on the larger section are not cut to a specific length — simply use the full width of the fabric, which may vary from 106 cm (42 inches) to 120 cm (47 inches).

Figure 2.3

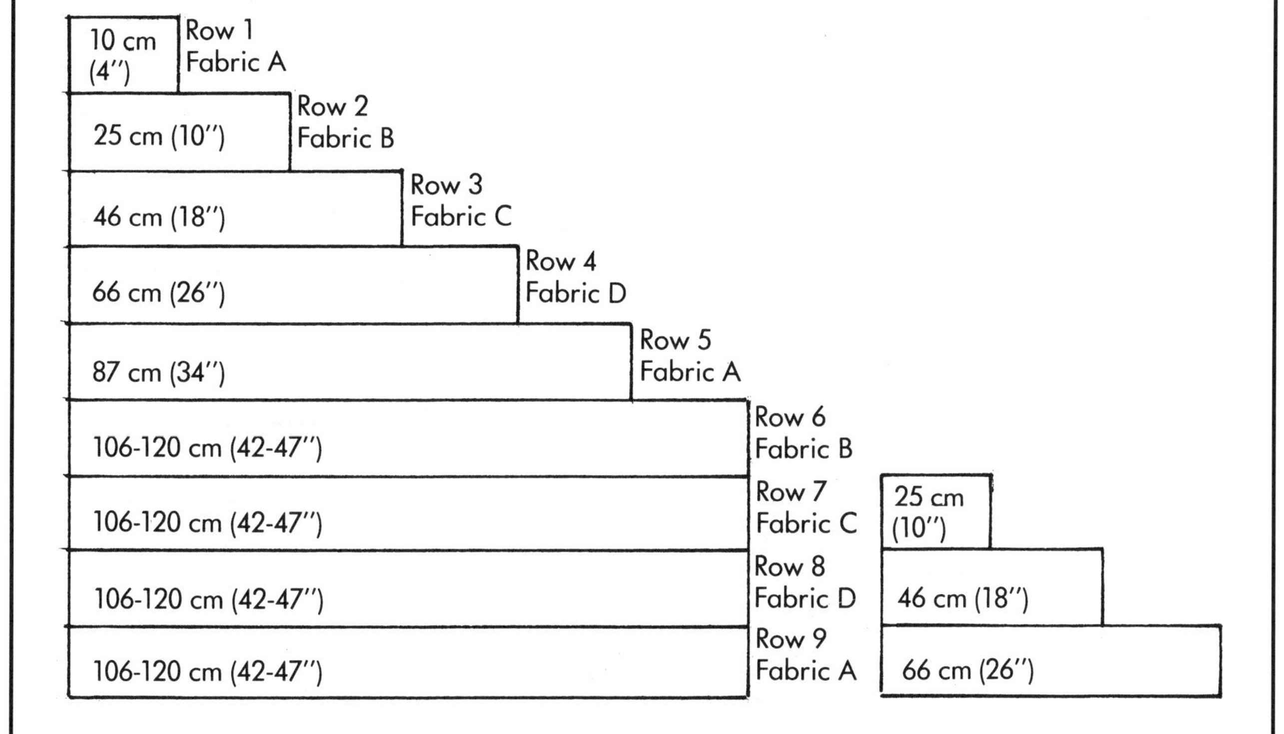

You may find it easier to lay out all the strips of fabric in order first, before sewing them, beginning with the long ones, then cutting the shorter ones to size.

The lengths of all strips allow a little extra (approximately 5 cm/2 inches) for uneven alignment of side edges and trimming of selvedges.

Step 3 — Re-cut the fabric 'steps' vertically in 2 inch widths, having first straightened up the left-hand side so that it is perpendicular to the seam lines and selvedges are removed. As the multitude of seams may cause some distortion, it is necessary to check after every few cuts that you are still on the perpendicular. (Figure 2.4)

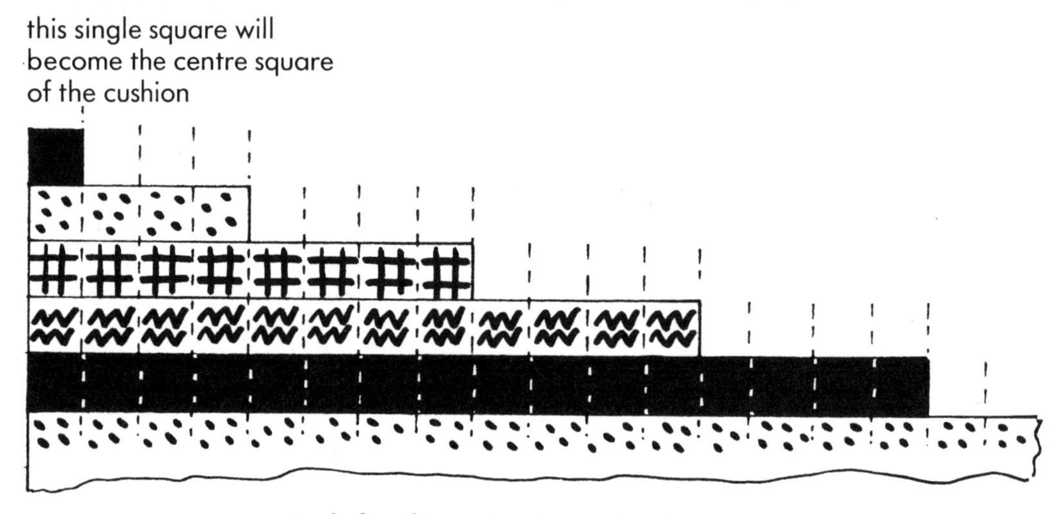

(only first five strips shown here)

Figure 2.4

Step 4 — Realign the strips of squares to form two halves of the cushion, starting with the longest strip in the centre and adding strips one square shorter on either side. You will be making up two pyramids at the same time, one slightly smaller than the other. (Figure 2.5). It is probably preferable to lay these out on the table or floor before attempting to sew them.

Iron seam allowances in opposite directions on alternate rows to enable seams to butt together (see Introduction) and make up the two pyramids.

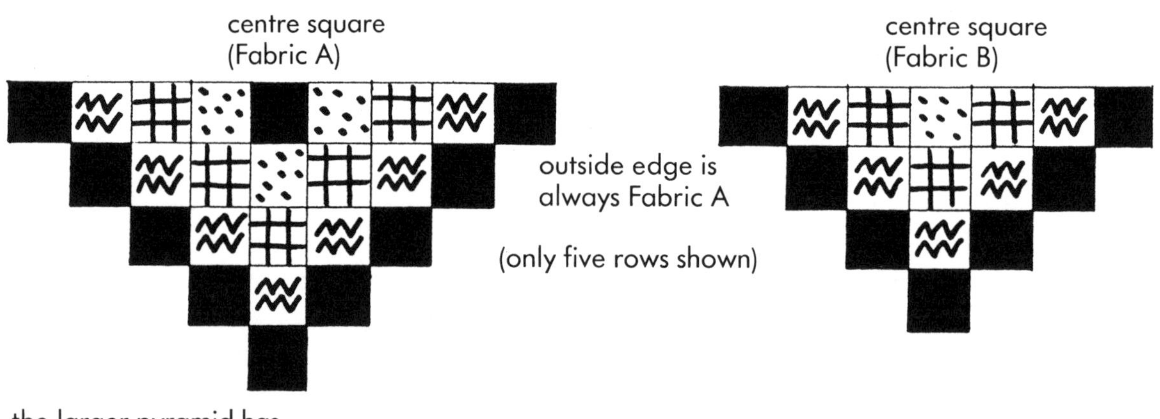

Figure 2.5

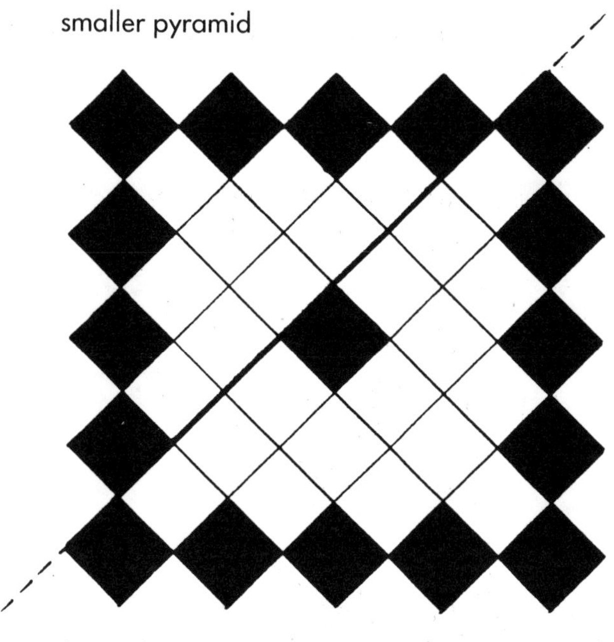

Figure 2.6

Step 5 — Finally, press these last seam allowances in opposite directions on each pyramid and join the two pyramids across the centre to form a square. (Figure 2.6)

Step 6 — *Making up the cushion*

Straighten off the sides of the square, leaving ¼ inch/6 mm seam allowance above the point of the last full diamond. (Figure 2.7)

You may wish to stay-stitch the outside edge along the seam line. (Figure 2.8)

Figure 2.7

Figure 2.8

To make the ruffle, cut three strips of fabric 6¼ inches wide across the full width of the fabric. Join the short ends together, then fold the ruffle in half along its length, wrong sides together (this method avoids the need to hem the outer edge of the ruffle). Gather the raw edges evenly and sew to the outside edge of the cushion top. Cushion centre should now measure approximately 43 cm (17 inch) square.

Make the cushion back, either with a zip set in or with overlapping flaps.

Join back cushion to front, right sides together, making sure ruffle is tucked inside away from stitching line. Sew from the pieced side of the cushion, along the stitching line used for the ruffle. Turn cushion to right side.

example shows six fabric reverse-repeat sequence

Figure 2.9 **Trip Around the World Quilt**

THE TRIP AROUND THE WORLD QUILT

The Trip Around the World quilt is pieced much like the cushion cover, but there is an additional centre section which will extend the shape into a rectangle.

The following instructions are for a single bed quilt measuring approximately 135 cm x 170 cm (53 inches x 67 inches). Borders measure 25 cm (10 inches).

There are two possible fabric sequences for this quilt. The first uses five fabrics, which are repeated once in the same sequence, before finally ending with the first fabric again. The second possible sequence uses six fabrics. These run in a reverse-repeat sequence, also ending with the first fabric.

REQUIREMENTS

1. For five fabric quilt
Fabrics run in a sequence A-E, repeated once and ending with a final A row (rows counted from centre of quilt outwards). (See plate 5)

Fabric A — 2.4 m (2⅝ yds) [includes 1.6 m (1¾ yds) for the border]

Fabrics B, C — 0.4 m (½ yd) each

Fabrics D, E — 0.5 m (⅝ yd) each

2. For six fabric quilt
Fabrics run in sequence A-F then reverse sequence, ending again with A. (Figure 2.9)

Fabric A — 2.1 m (2⅜ yds) [includes 1.6 m (1¾ yds) for border]

Fabrics B, C, D, E — 0.4 m (½ yd) each

Fabric F — 0.3 m (⅜ yd)

METHOD

Step 1 — Using the rotary cutter and the five or six different fabrics, cut 3 inch strips horizontally across the full width of the fabric. You will need:

For a five fabric quilt:
Fabric A — 7 strips
Fabric B — 4 strips
Fabric C — 5 strips
Fabric D — 6 strips
Fabric E — 6 strips

OR

For a six fabric quilt:
Fabric A-E — 5 strips each
Fabric F — 3 strips

Step 2 — Cut and join fabric strips as indicated below (Figure 2.10), aligning fabrics on the left-hand edge. Note that after the first three rows you will have to join additional strips separately as fabric will not be wide enough to form the 'steps'. There is no need to join these three sets of 'steps' to each other. Where the length of the strip states 'full width of fabric (106 cm/42 inches+)' this simply means to use the whole horizontal strip of fabric no matter what its length — there is no need to cut it. Fabrics may well vary in width from 106 cm (42 inches) to 120 cm (47 inches).

Mark your fabric sequence on the plan below:

Row	**1**	**2**	**3**	**4**	**5**	**6**	**7**	**8**	**9**	**10**	**11**
five fabric quilt	A	B	C	D	E	A	B	C	D	E	A
OR											
six fabric quilt	A	B	C	D	E	F	E	D	C	B	A

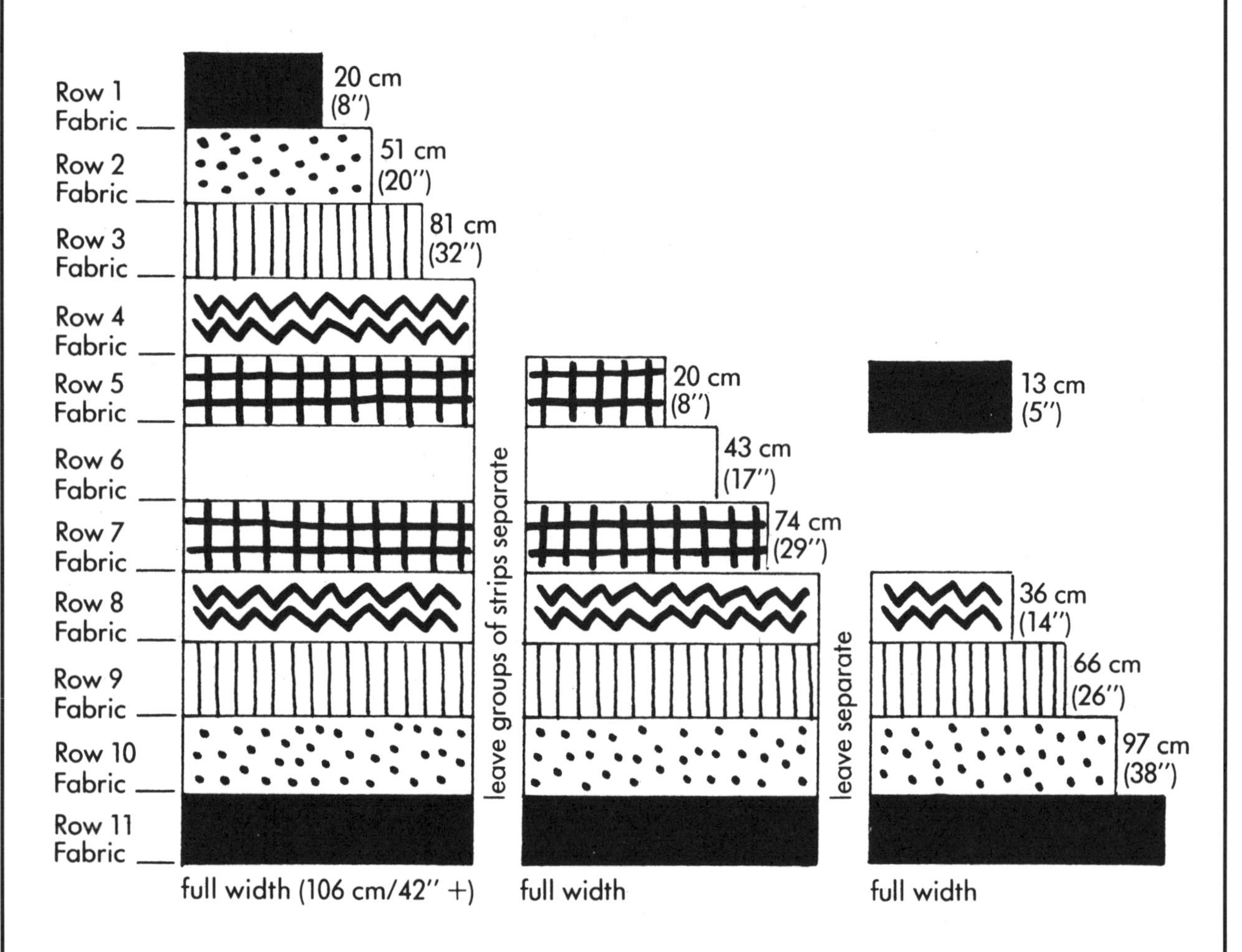

fabrics shown mimic the colour sequence in Figure 2.9, a six fabric reverse-repeat sequence

five fabric quilts will use a different sequence

Figure 2.10

These lengths allow a little extra (approximately 5 cm/2 inches) for uneven alignment of side edges and trimming of selvedges.

Iron all seam allowances in one direction.

Step 3 — Re-cut the fabric 'steps' vertically in 3 inch widths, having first trimmed up the left-hand side so that it is perpendicular to the seam lines, and the selvedges are removed. (Figure 2.11)

You should have two vertical strips with the centre colour at the top. The next four strips will have the second colour, the next four will have the third, and so on, until you end up with the four single 3 inch squares of the outside colour.

these two squares will become the centres of the two corner "pyramids"

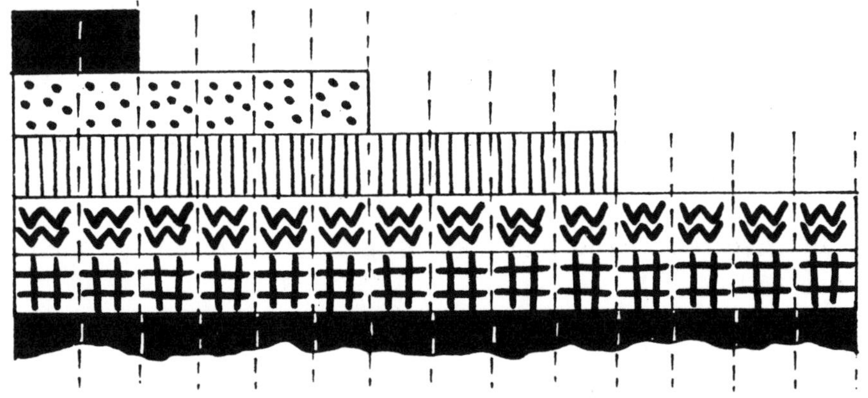

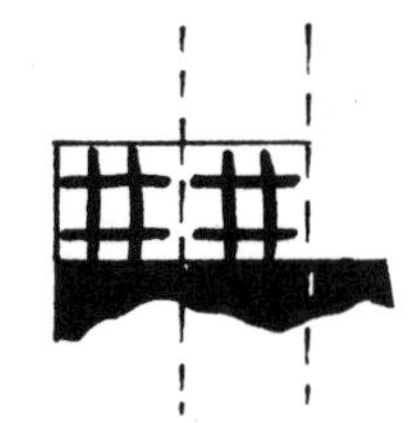

(first five rows only shown here)

Figure 2.11

Remember while you are cutting that the 'steps' may be slightly distorted from sewing and that the left-hand side may need trimming regularly, after every few cuts.

Step 4 — Realign the strips of squares to form the top and bottom corners of the quilt, starting with the longest strips in the centre and adding strips one square shorter on either side (Figure 2.12). You will be making up two pyramids like this at the same time.

(first five rows only shown here)

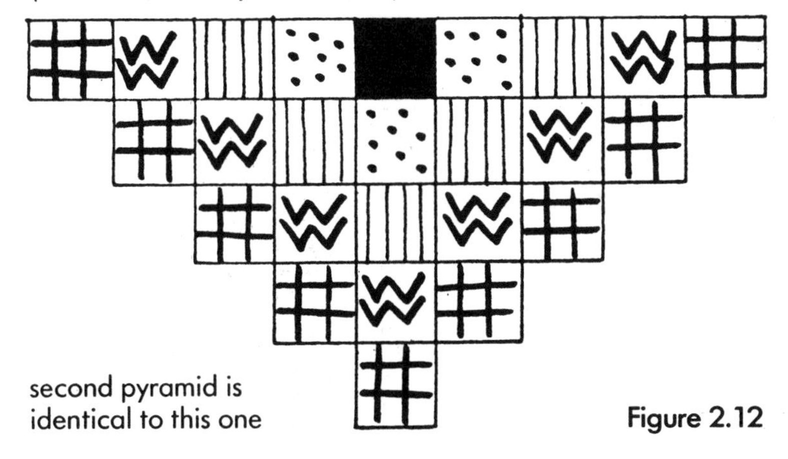

Figure 2.12

Before sewing together the strips which form the pyramids, iron the seam allowance in opposite directions on alternate rows. This will avoid bulky joins.

These two pyramids, when made up, form the top and bottom corners of the quilt. (Figure 2.13)

Figure 2.13

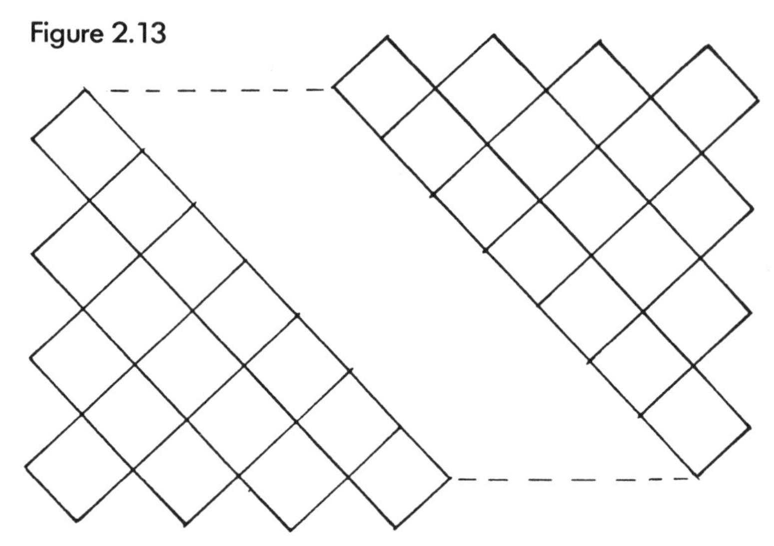

Step 5 — To make the centre section of the quilt, join 14 inch strips of fabric, 3 inches wide, as indicated below. (Figure 2.14)

Figure 2.14

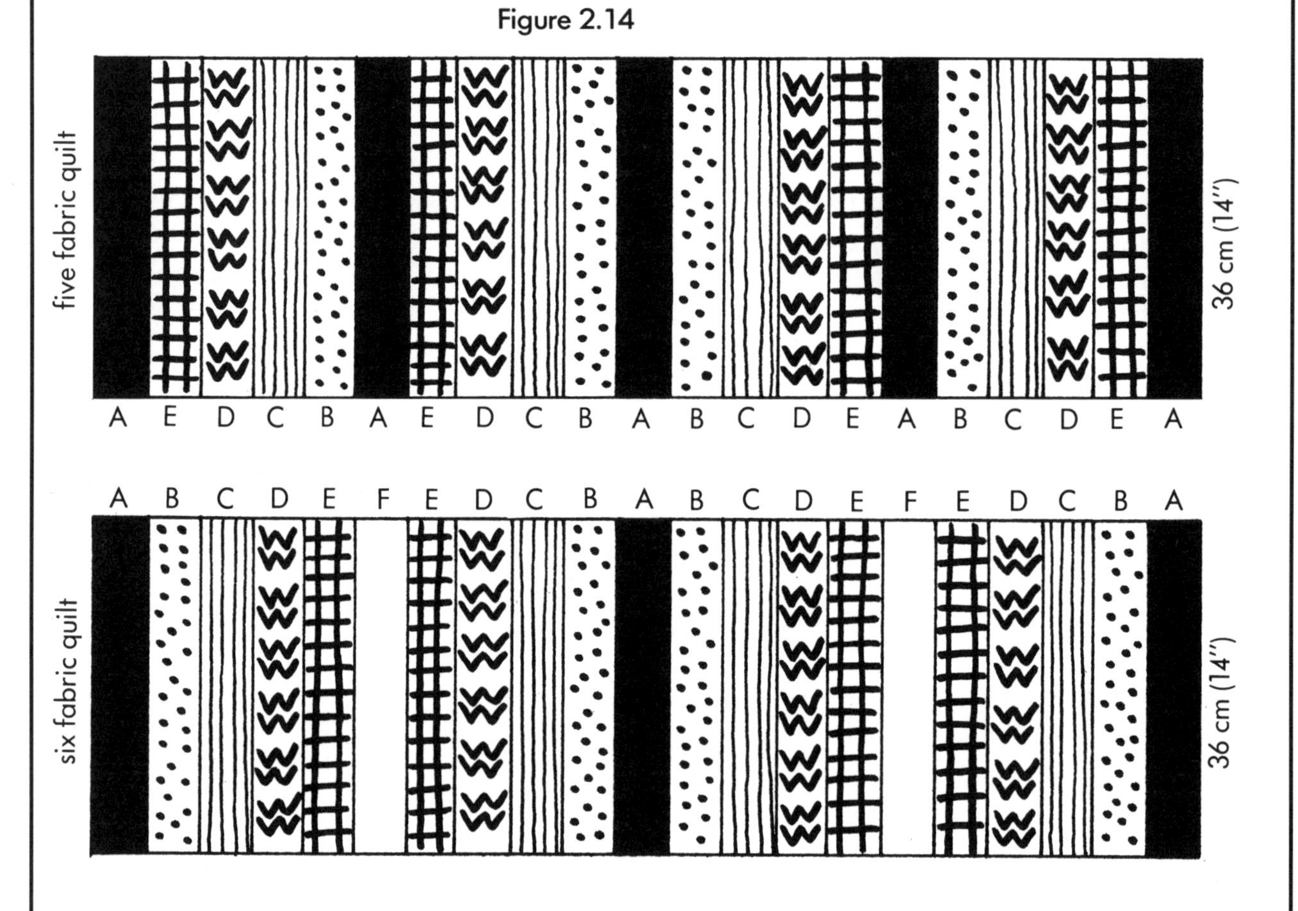

Re-cut these sections horizontally in 3 inch strips (you will get four strips from the 14 inch lengths). Press seam allowance in opposite direction on alternate rows and realign strips, shifting each row one square along. Rejoin rows. (Figure 2.15)

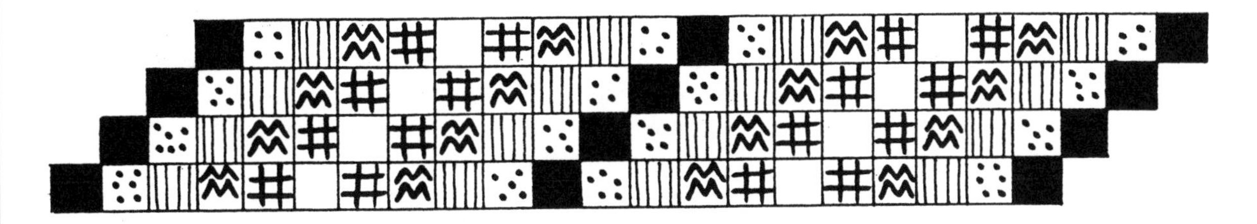

Figure 2.15

Step 6 — Join corner pyramids to each end of centre section to form quilt top. (Figure 2.16)

You are now ready to add the border — see Chapter 6.

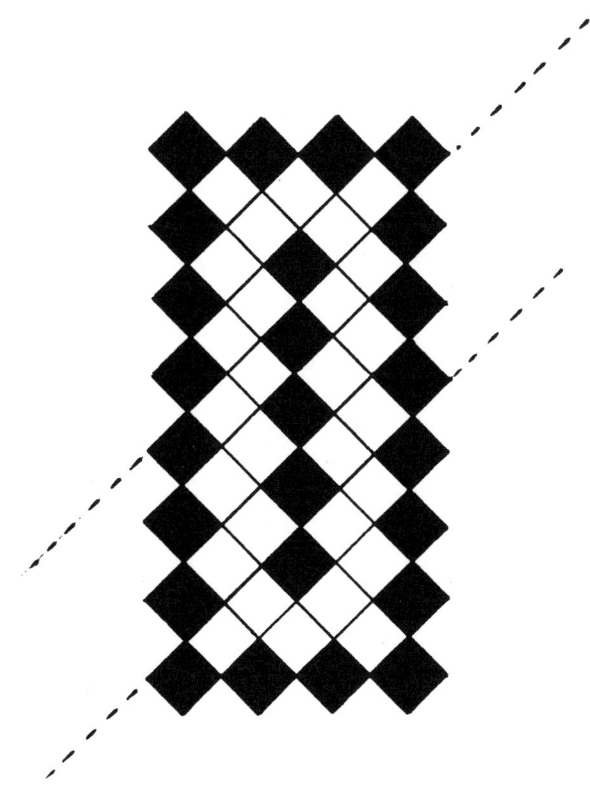

Figure 2.16

WAYS TO VARY THE SIZE OF THE QUILT

In the Trip Around the World piecing method, the *width* of the quilt is determined by the number of rows in the two pyramids which form the corner sections, while the *length* of the quilt is determined by the number of rows in the centre section.

To make a wider quilt, add extra rows, in the required colour sequence, to the pyramid sections. Each row will be 12 inches/30 cm (or the size of four squares) longer than the preceding row or 'step'.

To make a longer quilt, cut longer strips for the centre section. Each additional 3 inches/7.5 cm will make the centre section one square longer. Remember that the colour sequence for the centre section will always be the same as the bottom edge of the pyramid.

The overall size of the quilt can also be altered by increasing or decreasing the size of the squares. Remember to be consistent throughout in the size of the strips you are cutting for both the 'step' section which forms the corners and for the centre section. You will also have to alter the length of the strips in the pyramid section accordingly — each successive strip is longer than the last by the size of four squares (in the example quilt each strip is 12 inches/30 cm longer, i.e. 4 x 3 inches). Similarly the strips for the centre section will have to be cut according to the size of squares required — in the example quilt they are 14 inches/ 36 cm long, i.e. four rows of 3 inch squares plus a 2 inch/5 cm tolerance. At the beginning of this section the instructions for a cushion cover used 2 inch strips of fabric throughout. The same dimensions, but with a centre section added to form a rectangle, would, with borders added, make an excellent cot quilt.

Borders can also be used to change the dimensions of the quilt considerably — see Chapter 6.

CHAPTER 3

LONE STAR QUILT

The Lone Star pattern, also known as the Star of Bethlehem, is a traditional Amish design which forms the centre of a square quilt. The Amish liked square quilts because they could be turned and used in any direction, thus extending their wear. However, instructions are included at the end of the chapter for making the quilt rectangular.

Figure 3.1 **Lone Star Quilt**

The following instructions are for a quilt measuring approximately 208 cm (82 inches) square. This comprises:

- Centre star — 148 cm x 148 cm (58 inches x 58 inches)
- First border — 5 cm (2 inches)
- Second border — 25 cm (10 inches)

The finished size of the quilt may be varied by altering the size of the borders, or by increasing the size of the background to the star.

Note — all measurements may vary slightly with individual variation in seam allowance.

This quilt uses six fabrics (A-F) in a reverse-repeat sequence (A-B-C-D-E-F-E-D-C-B-A) for your star points, and a different fabric for the background. You may wish to frame the quilt with a border in one of the star fabrics, or allow the star to 'float' by continuing the background fabric into the border. (Figure 3.2)

Fabric B

Figure 3.2

star with multiple borders

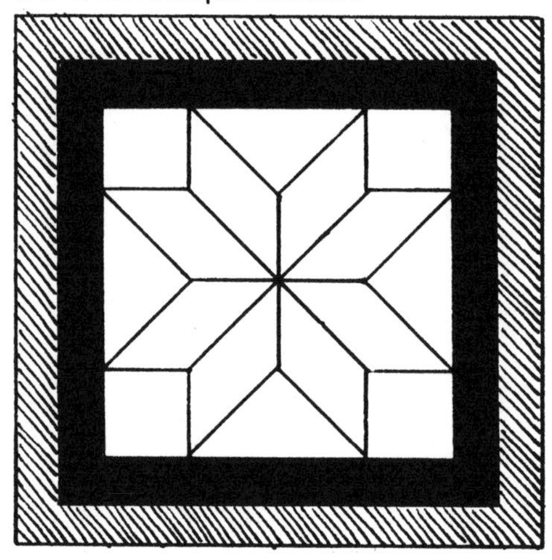

borders and background of one colour

Consult some books on Amish quilts or Judy Martin's *Shining Star Quilts* for inspiration. The off-cuts from the star piecing can be used very effectively in a narrow border. (See plates 12-16).

The cutting techniques for the Lone Star are slightly different to those used in the preceding two chapters because you will be making some of the cuts at a 45° angle, so before beginning, make sure you are familiar with the instructions in the Introduction. If your cutting board does not have a 45° angle marked on it, put one on using a permanent felt or light-projector pen, and start from the bottom left-hand corner. (Figure 3.3)

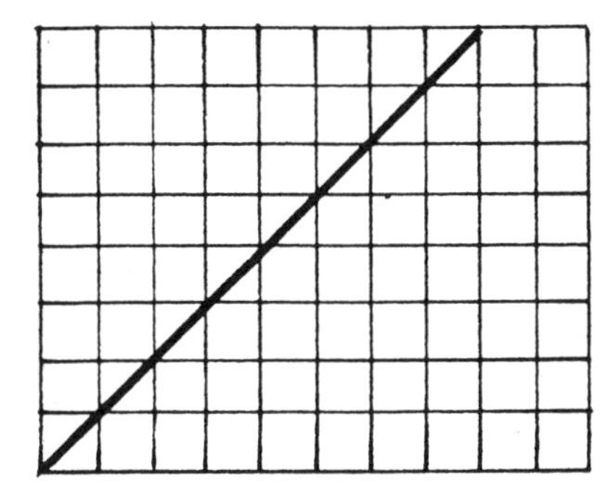

Figure 3.3

Figure 3.4 shows one of the eight star points with the six fabrics in reverse-repeat sequence.

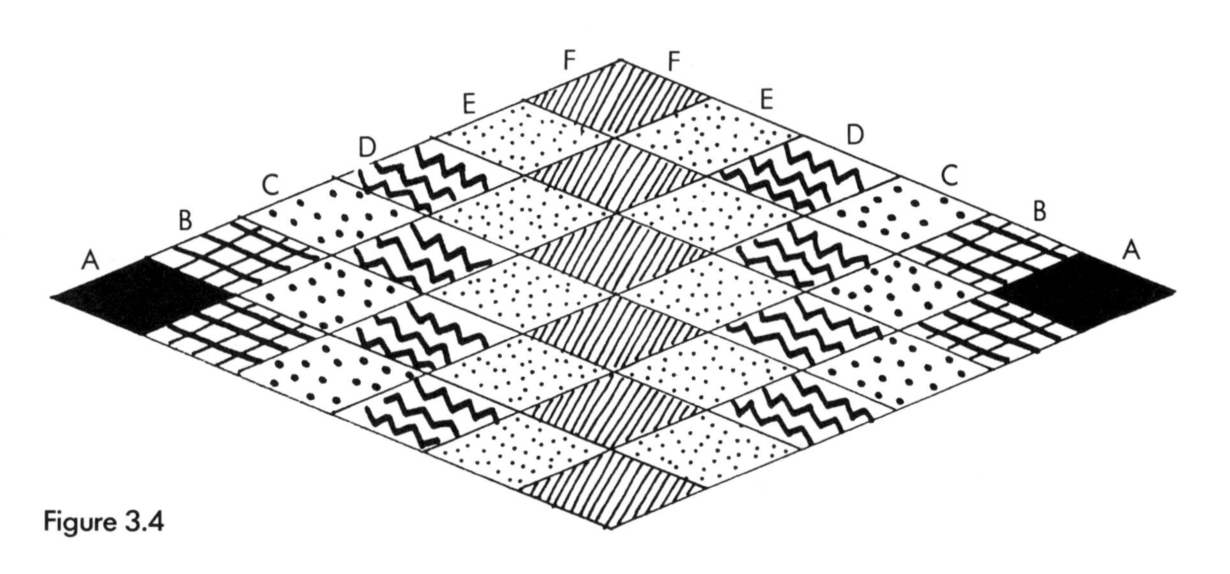

Figure 3.4

REQUIREMENTS

Fabric A — 20 cm (1/4 yd)
Fabric B — 30 cm (3/8 yd)
Fabric C — 50 cm (5/8 yd)
Fabric D — 60 cm (5/8 yd)
Fabric E — 80 cm (7/8 yd)
Fabric F — 50 cm (5/8 yd)

Background fabric

You may wish to leave the choice of your background fabric until after you have pieced the star, so that it can be tried against various background fabrics. It is difficult to visualise the colours of the star until it has been fully pieced, and you may find your preconceived ideas for a background fabric change when you see the completed star. Avoid using one of the fabrics in the star (fabrics A-F) in the background, as it will cause the matching section of the star to 'bleed' into the background, giving the impression that this part of the star is missing. (Figure 3.5)

Figure 3.5

You will require 1.6 metres (1¾ yds) of background fabric to set the star into its background square. This will give you the initial centre star before the borders are added.

Border fabric — See page 44, regarding your choice of border fabric.

For a 5 cm (2 inch) first border you will need 1.7 metres (1⅞ yds), or you can use the multicolour off-cuts from the star piecing (see plates 12-16). For the 25 cm (10 inch) second border you will need 2.2 metres (2½ yds). You may find the choice of border fabric is easier if left until after the star has been pieced and set into its background.

Note that these fabric quantities are for a square quilt measuring approximately 208 cm (82 inches) square. To make a different sized quilt, consult the notes on 'altering the quilt size' at the end of this chapter.

METHOD

Step 1 — *Strip piecing*

Using the rotary cutter, cut 2½ inch strips across the full width of the fabric as follows, following the instructions for cutting and piecing in the Introduction.

Fabric A — 2 strips
Fabric B — 4 strips
Fabric C — 6 strips
Fabric D — 8 strips
Fabric E — 10 strips
Fabric F — 6 strips

Join together units of strips as indicated below (Units 1-6) using a ¼ inch/6 mm seam allowance. To avoid the pieced units becoming curved, sew each strip from the opposite direction to the one before. (See Introduction, page 8).

Note — strips should be staggered back by approximately 2 inch/5 cm each row to allow for subsequent 45° angle cuts. (Figures 3.6-3.11)

Iron all seam allowances in one direction on each unit — if you iron Units 1, 3 and 5 one way and Units 2, 4 and 6 the other, it will enable diamonds to butt together neatly when the star points are joined.

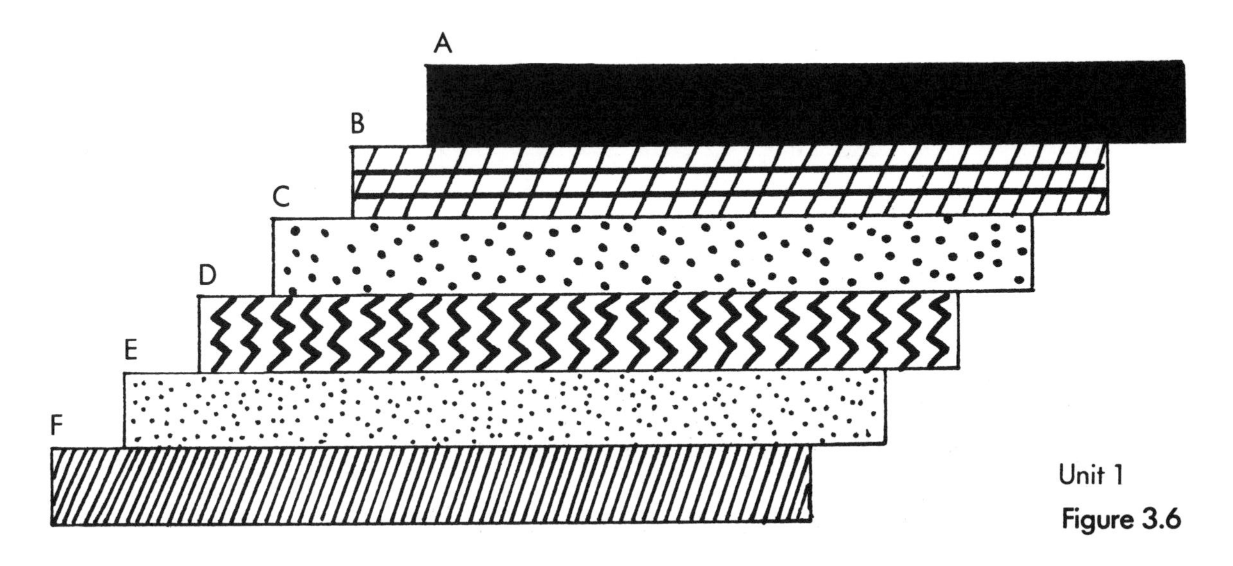

Figure 3.6

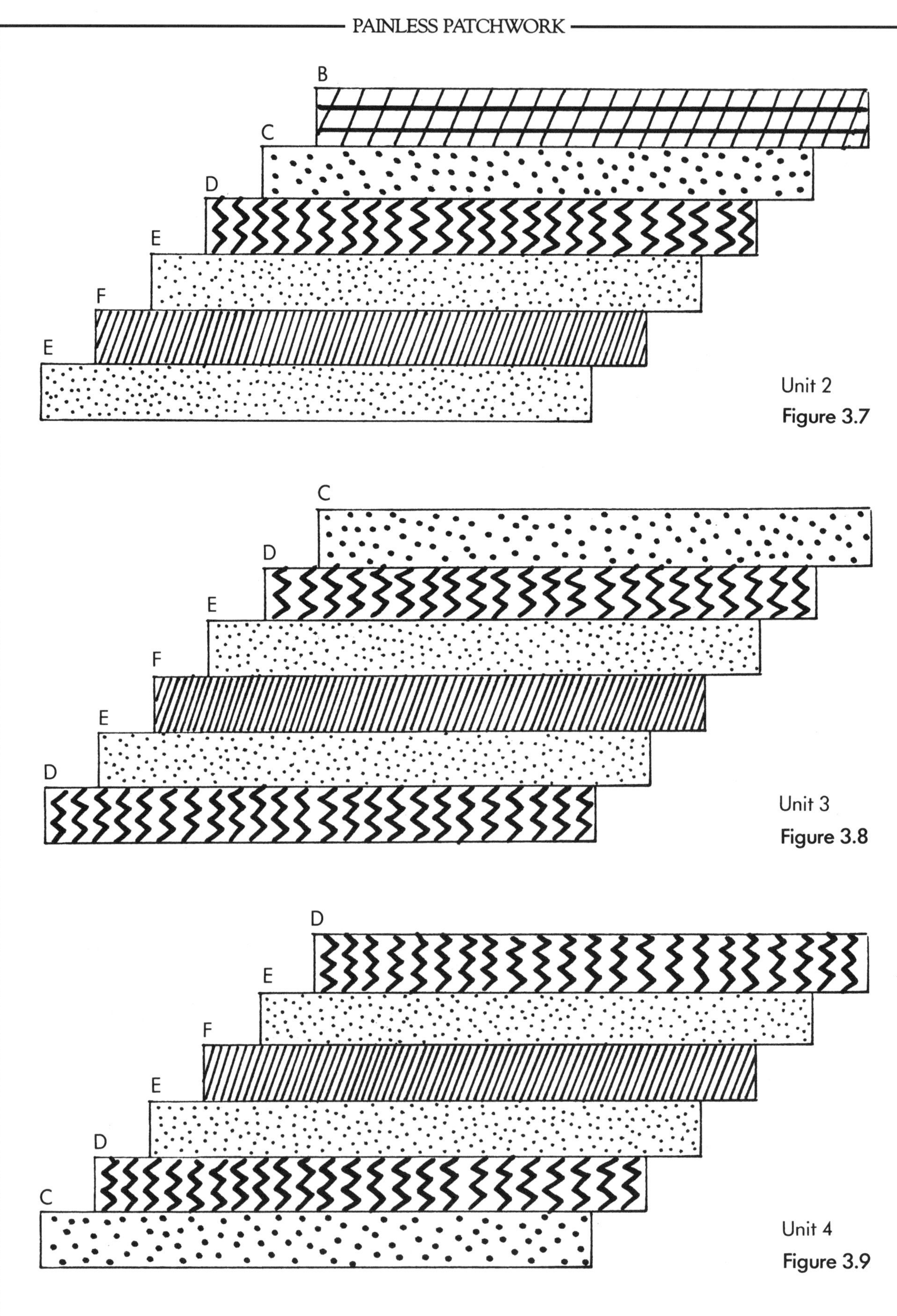

Unit 2
Figure 3.7

Unit 3
Figure 3.8

Unit 4
Figure 3.9

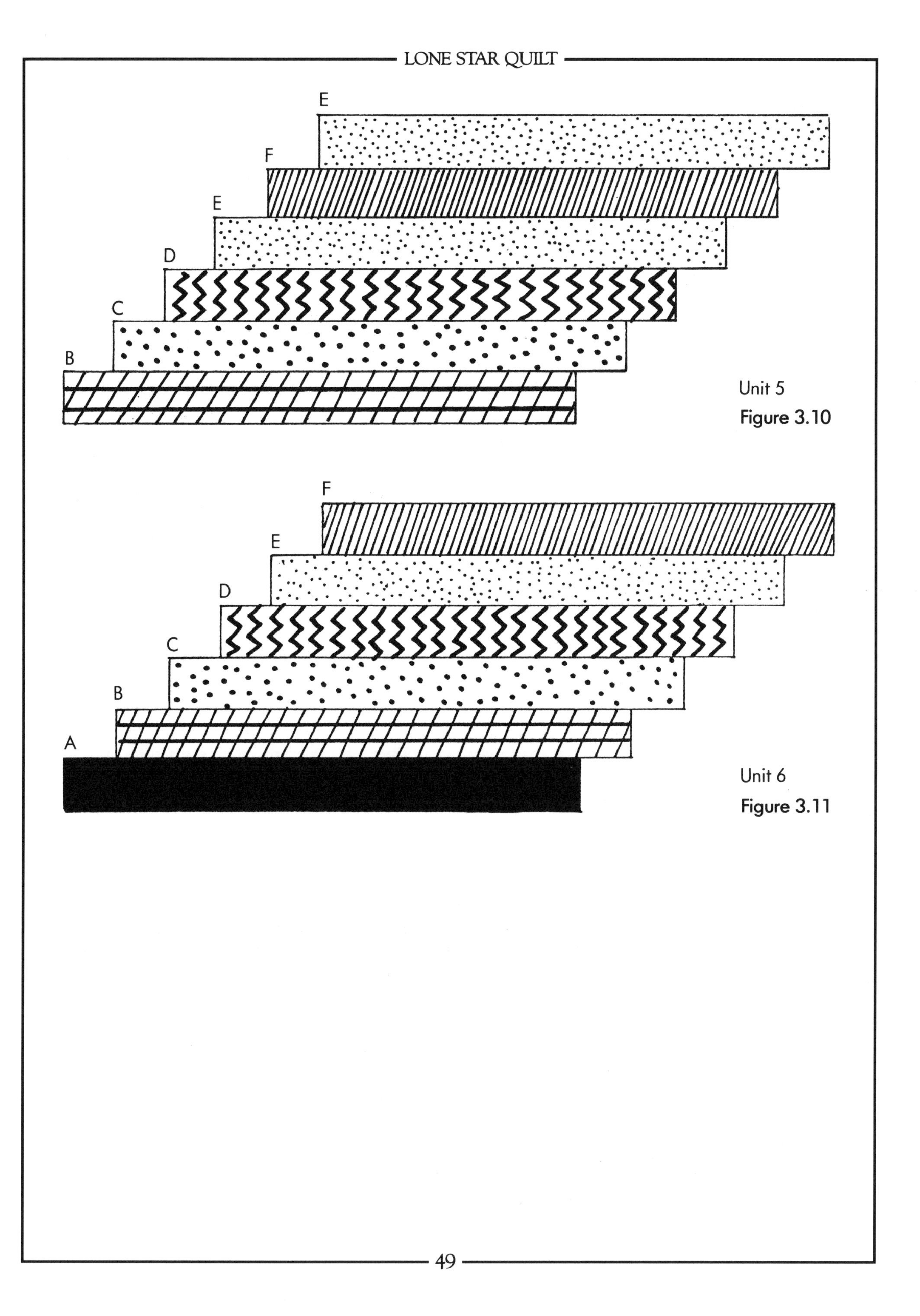

Figure 3.10

Figure 3.11

Step 2 — *Re-cutting the pieced units*
Now re-cut Units 1-6 in 2½ inch strips using the 45° angle mark on your board. Be sure that the seam lines follow the horizontal lines on the board before cutting the 45° angle, and check the alignment as you continue to cut strips — you may have to do this after each cut, trimming up the angled edge each time. (Figure 3.12)

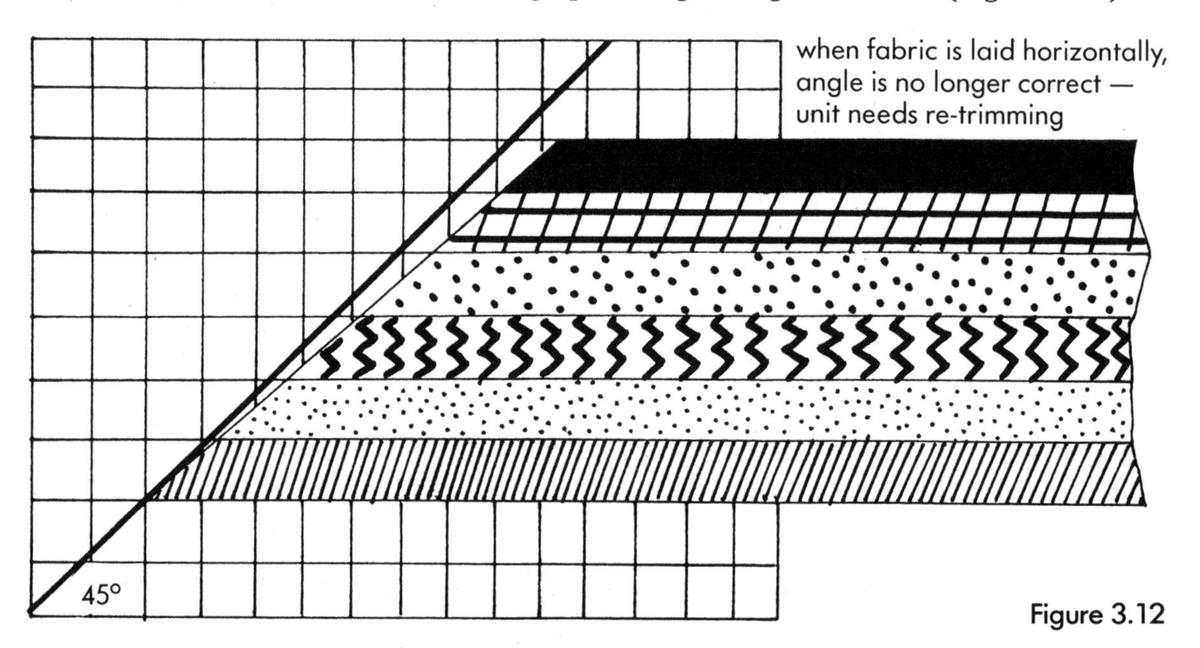

Figure 3.12

Cut carefully, remembering that you are cutting on the bias, where fabric has most stretch.

Cut 8 strips from each unit. Label these 'Unit 1', 'Unit 2', etc. (Figure 3.13)

Note — you will still have a reasonable amount left of each of these units, which you may wish to use later for the narrow 5 cm (2 inch) pieced first border. If you plan to do this, keep cutting until you run out of fabric, and put these extra strips aside for the border.

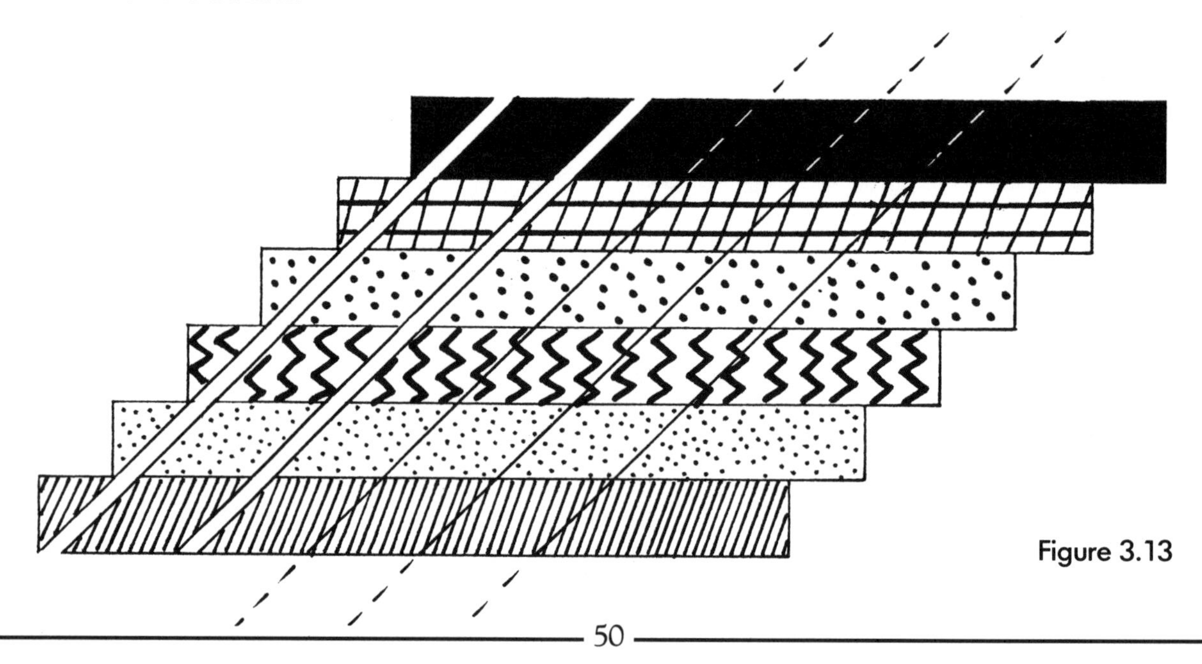

Figure 3.13

Step 3 — *Joining the angled strips into star points*
Taking one strip from each of Units 1-6, join these together to form the first star point. (Figure 3.14)

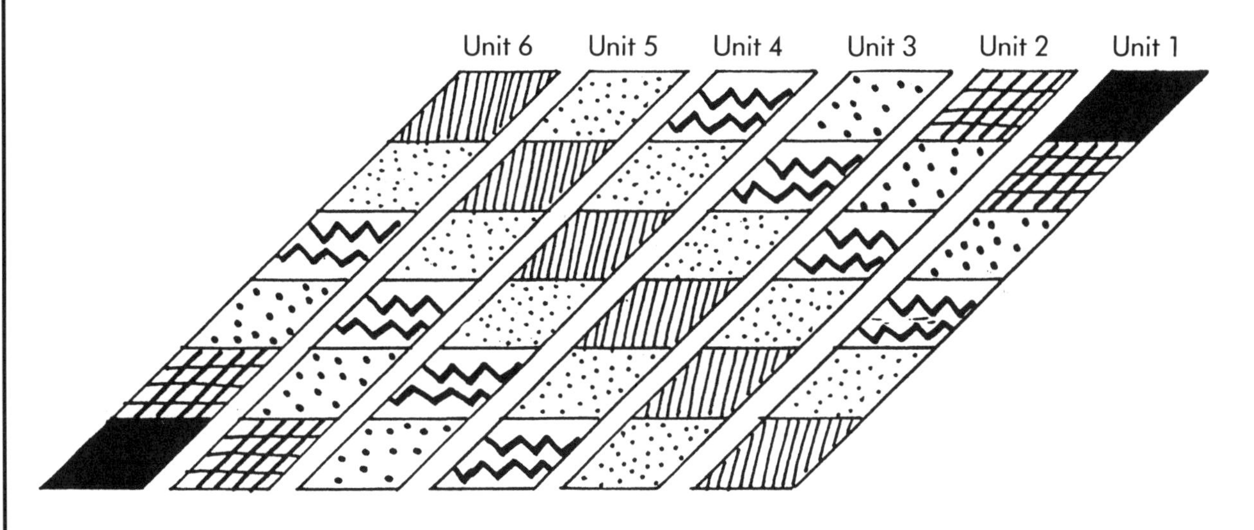

Figure 3.14

Remember to sew in alternate directions to avoid distorting the point. Having the seam allowance pressed in opposite directions on alternate rows will avoid bulky joints and assist diamonds to butt together neatly. However, making the diamond points meet neatly is not as easy as with square cut designs like the Double Irish Chain — because the seams on the Lone Star strips meet at an angle, they cannot be easily butted together. You will have to use a system of estimating by eye where the stitching line will be, then putting in a pin from the upper to the lower strips, through the points where the diamonds will meet on the seam line. If you use fine brass pins and put them in perpendicular to the stitching line you can sew — carefully! — over them to avoid any shift along the bias edges. Heavier pins will have to be removed just before the pressure foot reaches them. (Figure 3.15)

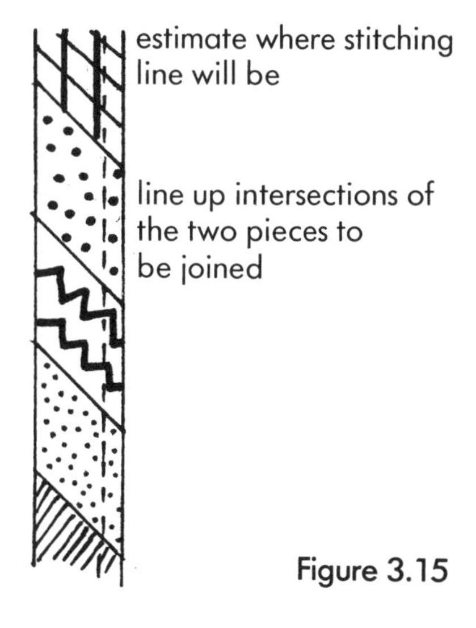

Figure 3.15

Repeat the process for the remaining seven star points.

Step 4 — *Joining eight star points to form the centre star*
Join four star points together, then another four, then join these through the middle, using pins throughout to make sure points meet. (Figure 3.16). Beware of unpicking if you make a mistake, particularly at the centre of the quilt. Bias edges can be easily stretched out of shape as you are joining them. Too much

unpicking and resewing can cause more damage than it fixes. You may find in some cases that slipstitching a section of a seam by hand causes less damage than getting the sewing machine back into a tricky spot and stretching fabric in the process.

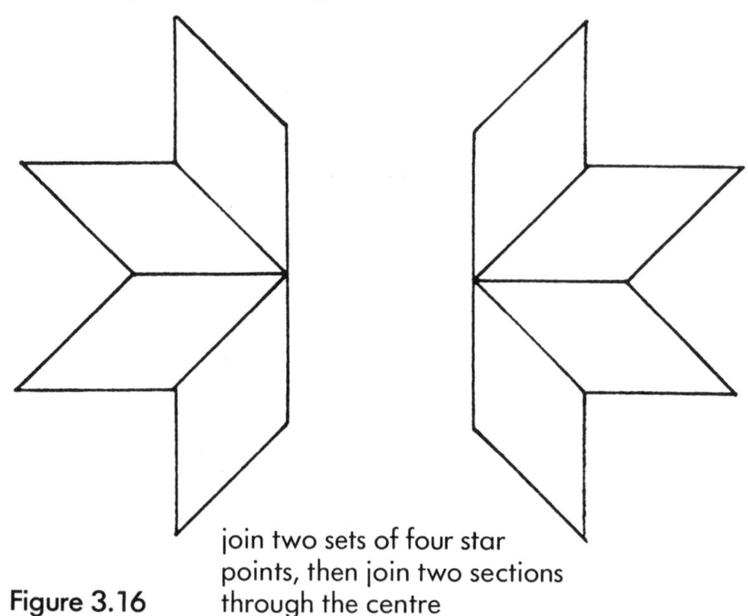

Figure 3.16 join two sets of four star points, then join two sections through the centre

Step 5 — *Cutting the background fabric*
Individual variance in piecing will mean that everyone's star is a slightly different size. It is important, therefore, before cutting out the background fabric, to measure your star points carefully, from the seam out to the tip (Figure 3.17) being very careful not to stretch the bias edge.

Figure 3.17

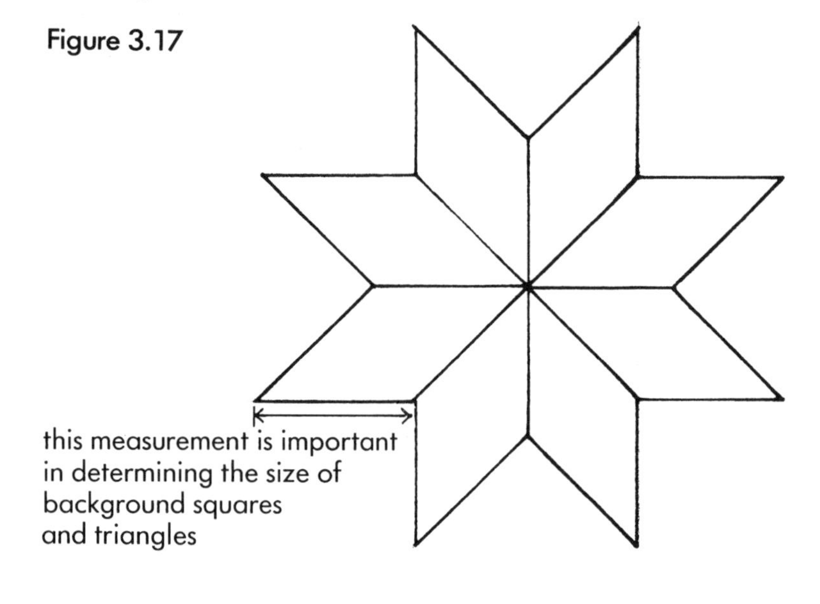

This measurement will determine the size of the squares and triangles which form the background to the star. Measure both edges of each star point. If they vary in length (as they may well do) decide on an average length, and use this for all your calculations. (If using a polyester fabric, decide on a measurement that is actually slightly above the average, as the polyester will have less give in it, and will not readily ease in the longer points.) The measurement of the star points is usually somewhere between 43 cm (17 inches) and 45 cm (18 inches). For this example, we will say the measurement is 44 cm (17½ inches).

Figure 3.18

i) The corner squares

The corner squares (Figure 3.18) will measure the same as the star points measurement you have just taken — in this example 44 cm (17½ inches). You will need to cut four squares this size from your background fabric. (Figure 3.19)

Figure 3.19

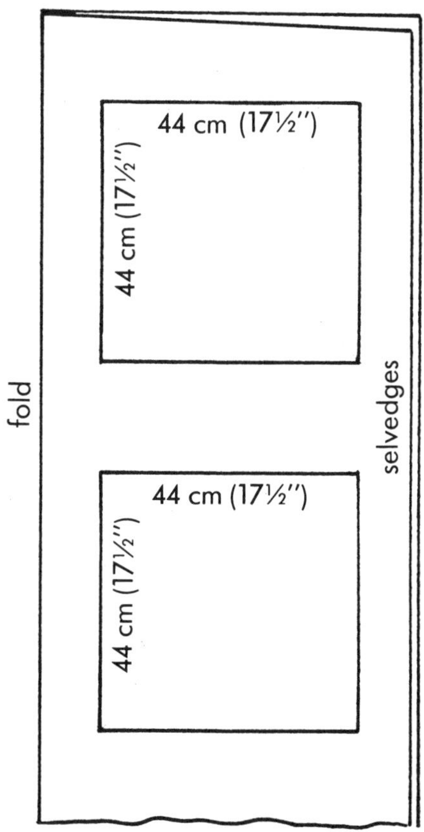

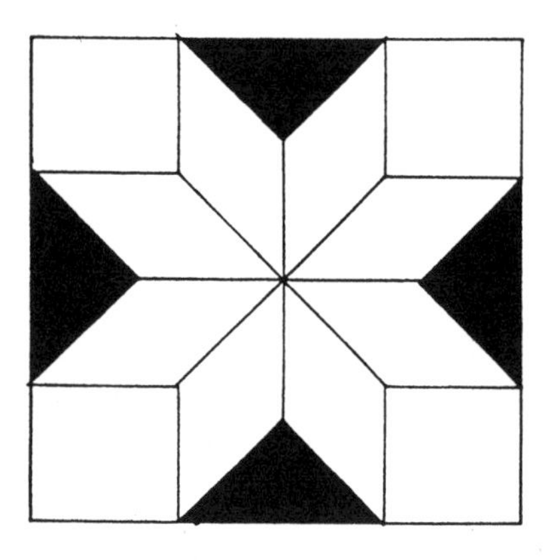

Figure 3.20

ii) The side triangles

These side triangles will have two sides adjoining the right angle which will measure 1 cm (½ inch) more than the sides of the background squares you have just cut. In the example, the squares were 44 cm (17½ inches) so the triangles will have to measure 45 cm (18 inches) on the two short sides. (Figure 3.21)

The four triangles can be cut out of one square of fabric, marked and cut diagonally, as shown below. (Figure 3.22)

To estimate the size of the square which will yield these four triangles, you will need a calculator with a $\sqrt{}$ button. The size of the square is $\sqrt{2\,(x+1)^2}$ (remember Pythagoras?). In our example, where the star points (x) measured 44 cm (17½ inches), the square for the four triangles will measure

$\sqrt{2(45)^2} = \sqrt{4050} = 63.6$ cm $\qquad \sqrt{2(18)^2} = \sqrt{648} =$ 25½ inches

But **don't panic!** If geometry and algebra is not your strong point, the chart on page 55 will help your calculations.

Figure 3.21

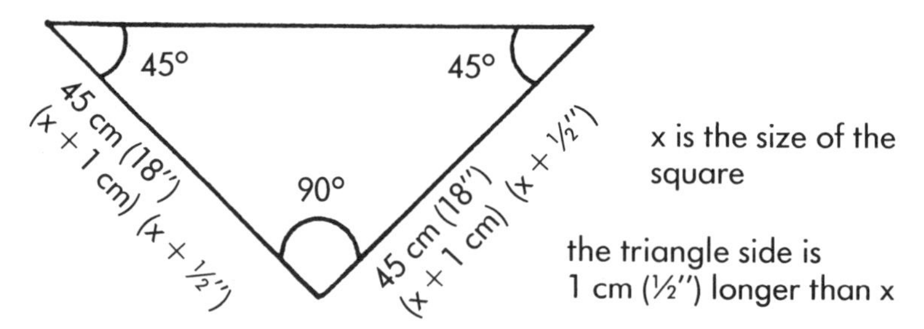

Figure 3.22

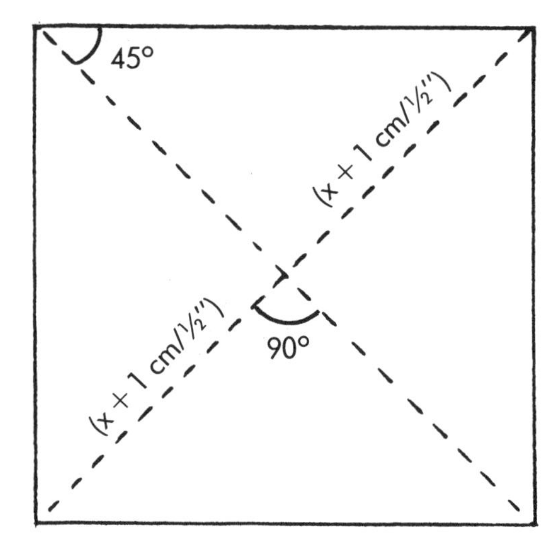

SOME LIKELY MEASUREMENTS FOR YOUR SIDE TRIANGLES (TO SAVE YOU CALCULATING)		
sides of star points measurement (average)	background squares (cut four)	squares from which to cut four triangles
42 cm	42 cm	60.8 cm
42.5 cm	42.5 cm	61.5 cm
43 cm	43 cm	62.2 cm
43.5 cm	43.5 cm	62.9 cm
44 cm	44 cm	63.6 cm
44.5 cm	44.5 cm	64.3 cm
45 cm	45 cm	65 cm
45.5 cm	45.5 cm	65.7 cm
46 cm	46 cm	66.4 cm
16½ inches	16½ inches	23⅜ inches
16¾ inches	16¾ inches	23¾ inches
17 inches	17 inches	24 inches
17¼ inches	17¼ inches	24⅜ inches
17½ inches	17½ inches	24¾ inches
17¾ inches	17¾ inches	25 inches
18 inches	18 inches	25½ inches
18¼ inches	18¼ inches	25¾ inches

Step 6 — *Piecing in the background fabric*
Pin one side of a corner square to one edge of a star point, beginning at the point where two star pieces join and working outwards. It helps to pin through the two at either end, matching the exact points where the seam allowances intersect. (Figure 3.23)

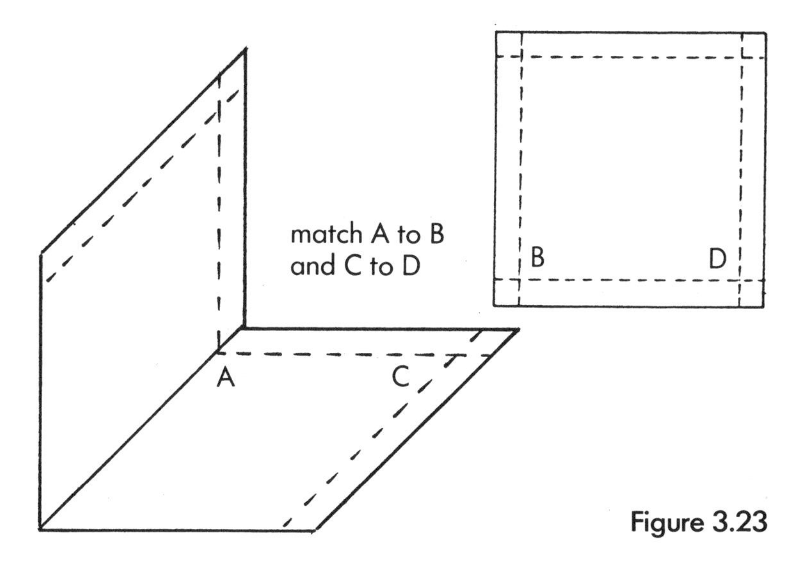

Figure 3.23

Be sure to start exactly where the two sections of the star meet, to avoid any tucks forming at this pivotal point. The tip of the star will extend beyond the edge of the square — this is quite normal where a square piece meets a triangular piece.

Begin again at the intersection of the two star pieces and sew the other side of the square to the adjoining star point. You may need to cut into the seam allowance of both the square and the star where they form a right angle. This will allow the square to be pivoted at this point. Use shorter stitches at the beginning of both of these seams to give extra strength to this pivotal point.

Repeat this process for the remaining squares and triangles. You should take extra care with the triangles, as both the star edges and the triangle edges are on the bias and therefore prone to stretching. The tips of the triangles will meet up exactly with the tips of the star (unlike the squares — see above).

You are now ready to add the borders — refer to the general instructions in Chapter 6. You may also wish to incorporate the piecing off-cuts into a narrow border (see plates 12-16).

Using the piecing off-cuts for a border
Continue cutting 2½ inch strips from the strip-pieced units that were used to make the star points. Join these into one long piece, then cut borders from this. Two matters should be noted regarding this pieced border:

i) The diamonds will form odd shaped pieces where they meet on the corners, even if these corners are mitred. (Figure 3.24)

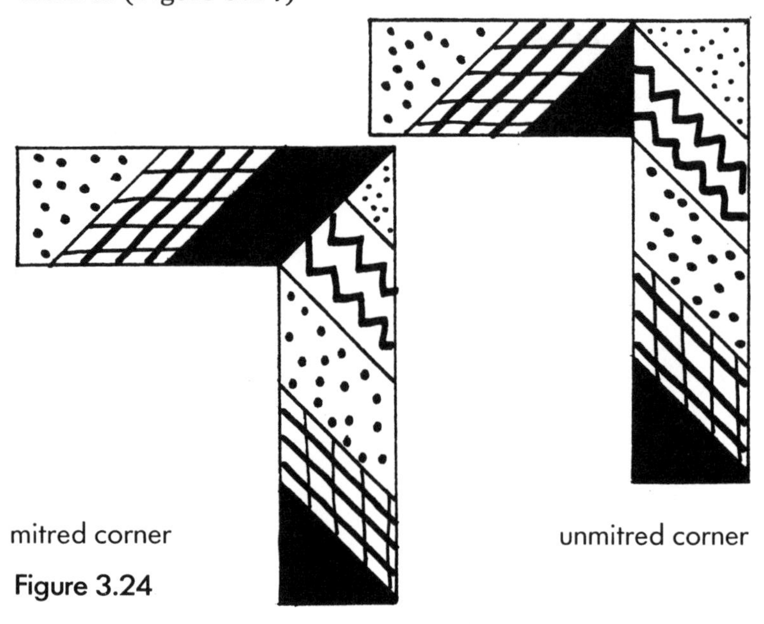

Figure 3.24

This problem (if it *is* a problem!) can be minimised by ensuring that the same fabric is on both sides of the corner, thus making the unusual joins less noticeable, and

ii) this pieced border has been cut on the bias. You must be *very* careful not to stretch the fabric when adding the pieced border to the quilt, and when adding the outer border to the pieced border. Stretching the pieced border when adding the outer border will result in a wavy border.

SOME VARIATIONS ON THE EXAMPLE QUILT

i) Making the square quilt into a rectangular quilt

Follow the instructions to the end of Step 6, where you have pieced in the background fabric. You will have a square measuring approximately 150 cm (59 inches) square. Now add some more of the background fabric to the top and bottom of the quilt, to create the effect that the star has been set into a rectangle. (Figure 3.25)

Now continue to add your borders to the quilt in the usual way. (Figure 3.26)

Additional fabric will have to be estimated, dependant upon the finished size of the quilt required.

Figure 3.25

Figure 3.26

ii) Other ways to vary the size of the quilt

The size of the quilt centre can be altered by using a different width strip for piecing and cutting the strip pieced units which make the star points.

For example, by cutting 2 inch strips throughout, instead of 2½ inch as in the example quilt, the star centre will measure approximately 110 cm (43 inches) square instead of 150 cm (59 inches) square.

The size of the star can be increased or reduced by altering the number of rows of diamonds in the star. The example quilt has eleven rows of diamonds in a reverse-repeat sequence — A-B-C-D-E-F-E-D-C-B-A. A four fabric reverse-repeat quilt (A-B-C-D-C-B-A) would be much smaller, having only seven rows of diamonds in the star points. You would only need to piece four units of strips for this. (Figure 3.27)

Figure 3.27

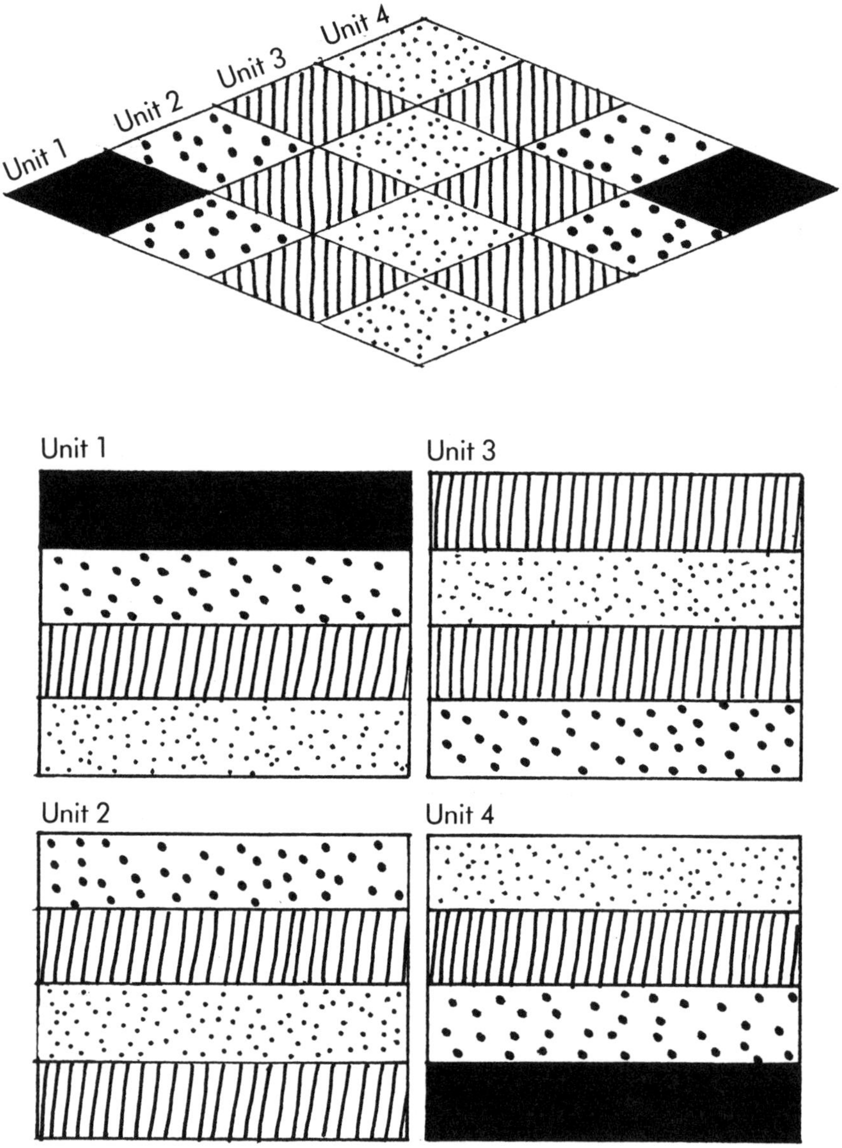
Unit 1
Unit 2
Unit 3
Unit 4
Unit 1
Unit 3
Unit 2
Unit 4

iii) Altering the colour sequence

Altering the colour sequence in the star is simple. Draw a plan of one star point (refer back to page 45 to help you) and mark in where you want each colour to be, then divide the point up into its respective strip piecing units. (Figure 3.28)

In this way you will be able to copy the colour sequence of any quilt you see in a book.

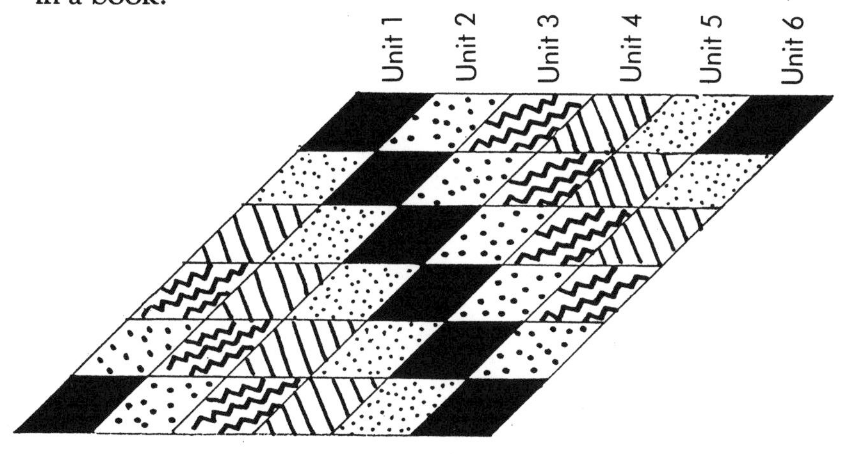

single repeat sequence
(A-B-C-D-E-A-B-C-D-E-A)

Figure 3.28

iv) More advanced settings

(*Note* — to simplify illustrations, each star point is shown as a single block of colour.)

One traditional variation on the Lone Star is the Broken Star. This requires the piecing of an *additional* 24 star points to surround the central star. (Figure 3.29). An outstanding example of this can be seen in A *Gallery of Amish Quilts* by Robert Bishop and Elizabeth Safanda (Dutton, 1976) plate 146, p. 89.

Figure 3.29

An interesting setting can also be created by replacing the four triangles in the background with four more squares. This requires a little more thought in piecing the border, but creates an interesting design. (Figure 3.30)

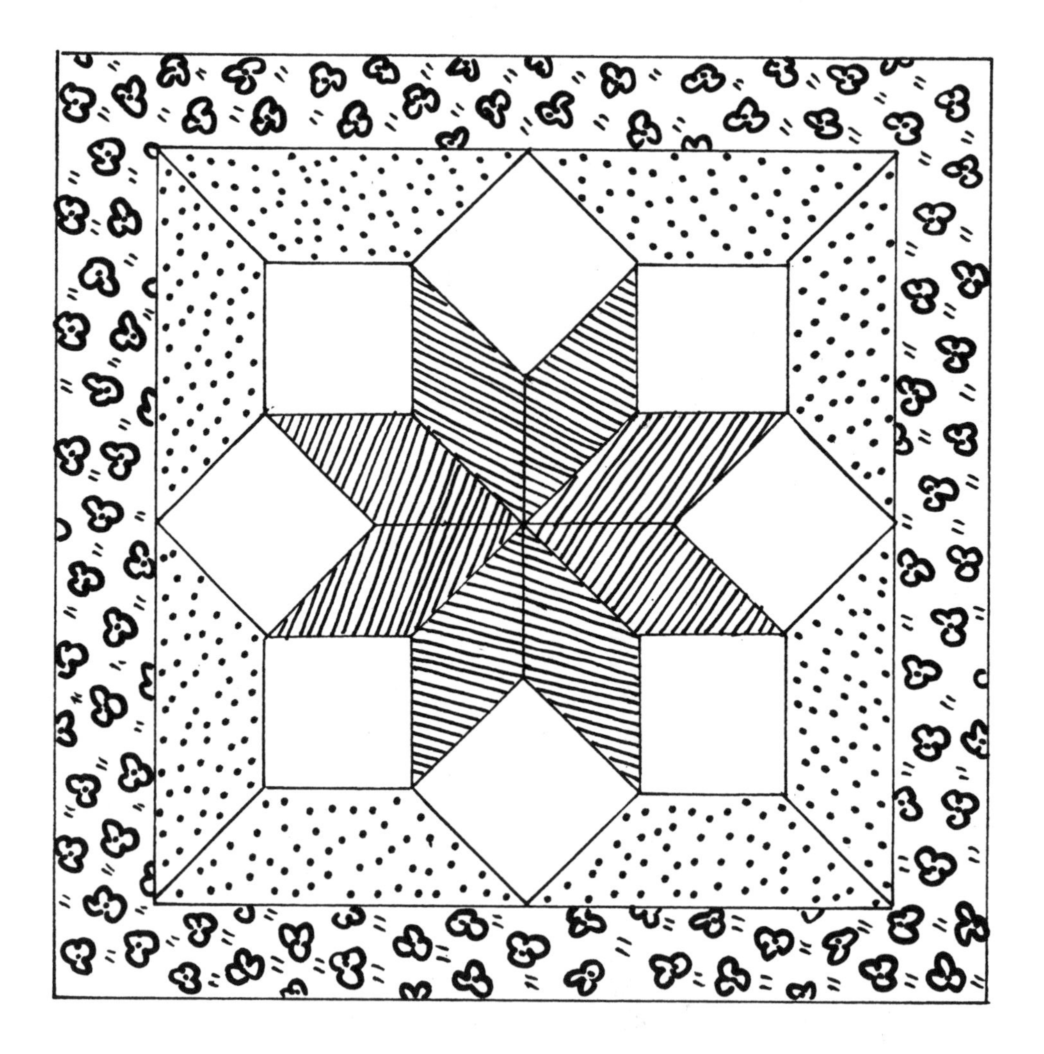

Figure 3.30

Both the size and look of the quilt can be changed by placing the square with the star on point, and adding triangles around it, much like the Amish Centre Diamond settings. (Figure 3.31) (See plate 13)

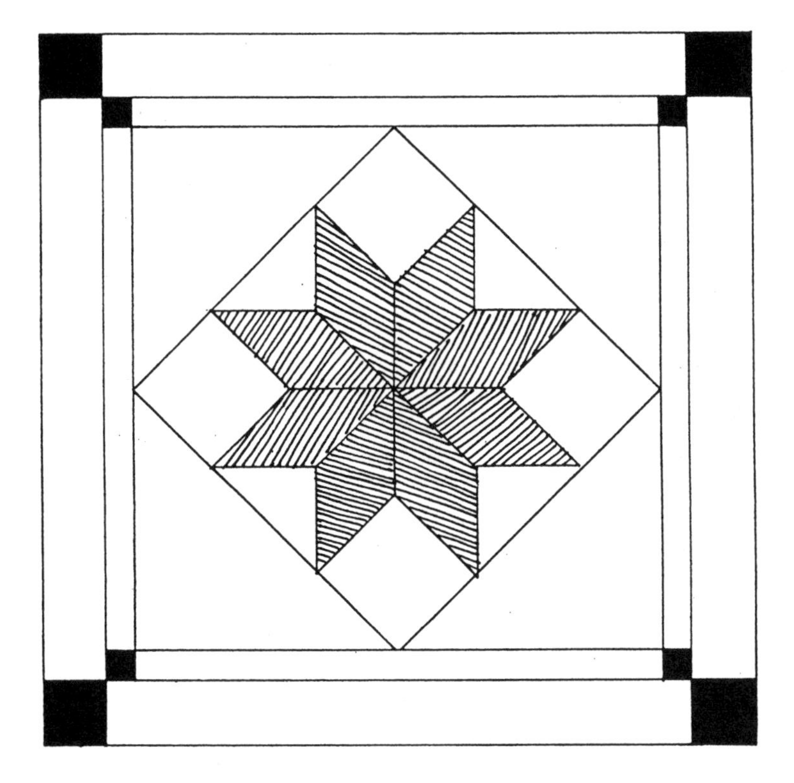

Figure 3.31

Figure 4.1 the Barn Raising design is just one of the many possible settings for Log Cabin blocks **Log Cabin Quilt**

CHAPTER 4

LAZY LOG CABIN

THE ESSENTIALS OF SPEED PIECING

This is an easy method of making a large number of Log Cabin blocks at one time, rather than piecing and completing blocks individually. I can't claim any rights to this method, which has been around for a long time, but in the second part of this chapter I will explain how it can be used creatively.

The traditional Log Cabin design works best when the fabrics are divided into light and dark groupings (Figure 4.2). These are then placed on opposite sides of the Log Cabin block and form patterns of light and shade across the quilt. Some of these overall shading designs are shown below. The same effect may be achieved by using different colours on each side of the block, e.g. green on one side, red on the other. (See plates 8 + 9)

a single Log Cabin block

Figure 4.2

Over the page are just a few of the many possible arrangements for Log Cabin blocks. (Figure 4.3). Virtually any patchwork design which features paired triangles (◪) can be adapted for Log Cabin settings.

overall quilt designs

each 0.5 cm (¼″) square represents a log cabin block with its light and dark sides

Figure 4.3

The following requirements are for a 48-block quilt (6 wide by 8 long) of identical blocks. The size may be altered by adding blocks in either direction, but note that some of the arrangements of blocks require an even number of blocks in both directions to be effective (e.g. Barn Raising). Others, such as Straight Furrows, are effective with odd or even numbers of blocks across or down the quilt. Blocks measure approximately 25 cm (10 inches) when finished.

You will need seven fabrics — three light, three dark, and one for the centre as illustrated in Figure 4.2 (or three each of two different colour groups, plus the centre). I have numbered the fabrics, from the centre out, light (L) 1, 2 and 3 and dark (D) 1, 2 and 3.

REQUIREMENTS

Centres — 40 cm (½ yd)
L(1) — 50 cm (⅝ yd)
L(2) — 80 cm (⅞ yd)
L(3) — 1.2 m (1⅜ yd)
D(1) — 70 cm (¾ yd)
D(2) — 1.0 m (1⅛ yd)
D(3) — 1.2m (1⅜ yd)

METHOD

Step 1 — Using the rotary cutter, cut horizontal strips across the full width of the fabric as follows, following the instructions for cutting and piecing in the Introduction.

Centre fabric — four 2¾ inch strips
Fabric L(1) — eight 1¾ inch strips
Fabric L(2) — fifteen 1¾ inch strips
Fabric L(3) — twenty-four 1¾ inch strips
Fabric D(1) — twelve 1¾ inch strips
Fabric D(2) — eighteen 1¾ inch strips
Fabric D(3) — twenty-four 1¾ inch strips

Lay the fabrics out in such a way that you can easily recognise where they will appear in the block.

Step 2 — Starting with the centre fabric and the first light (L1) fabric, sew together along one side, using a ¼ inch/6 mm seam allowance. (Figure 4.4)

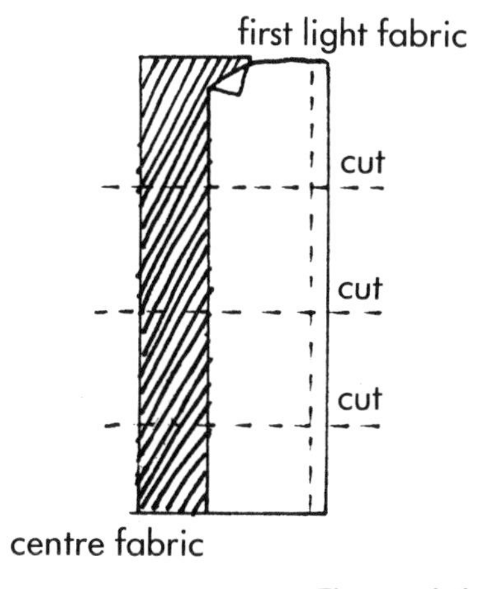

Figure 4.4

Step 3 — Square off the end of these double strips then cut through them every 2¾ inches. You may have to square off the end several times as the strips can become distorted from sewing. You will need 48 of these paired pieces, or one for every block you are making. Finger press open these paired pieces with the seam allowance towards the L1 strip. These form the centre and first side of your 48 log cabin blocks. From now on you will be adding successive strips to these centres all at the same time, in a sort of 'washing line' fashion.

Step 4 — Take another strip of the same light fabric you have just used. Sew this to the second side of the blocks you have just begun (Figure 4.5), making sure as you work that:

i) the strip you are adding is on the bottom (right side up) and

ii) the blocks are on top of it (right side down) and
iii) the last strip you added is at the top of the block (closest to the needle) and the seam allowance from that strip also faces the top of the block.

By following these rules you will be adding onto the correct side of the block and cannot throw the colours out of sequence and all the seam allowances will face towards the outside of the block and will not overlap each other (Figure 4.5). Separate the blocks.

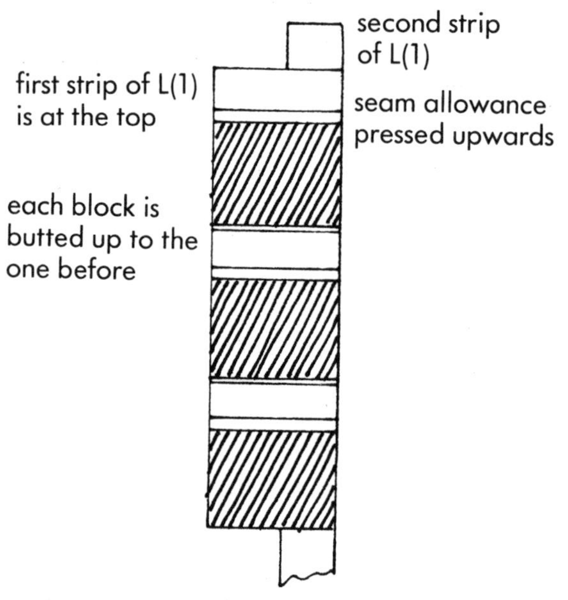

Figure 4.5

Figure 4.6

splayed out seam will make this side of the block longer and throw it off-square

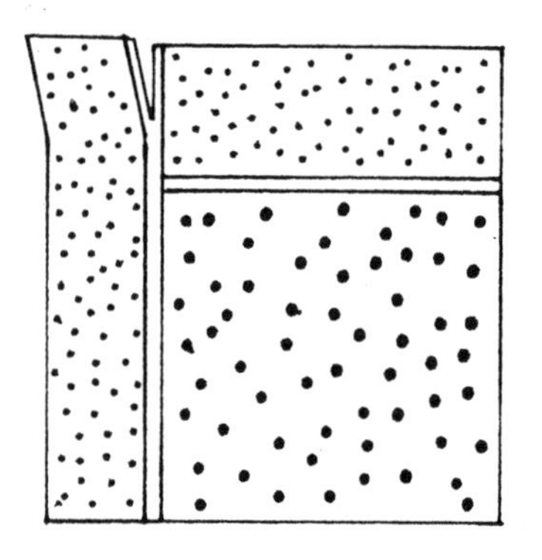

Step 5 — Add the first dark fabric to the next two sides, still following the rules stated above, then return to the second light fabric, then the second dark, and so on until all six fabrics have been added.

Because of the number of seams in the Log Cabin block there is a tendency for it to go off square. This can largely be avoided by ensuring that the seam allowance is consistent throughout and, more importantly, by taking care that the ends of seams do not unraval and splay out as you add each new strip. (Figure 4.6). For this reason it is advisable to use a shorter stitch length for the Log Cabin blocks.

Another point to be aware of as you separate the blocks each time is that the new strip is trimmed off square with the block. (Figure 4.7)

To summarise the speed piecing method for Log Cabin, there are *four rules to remember when piecing the blocks:*

a) Place the strip you are adding, right side up, on the bottom and the blocks on top, right side down.
b) The last strip you added should be facing up towards the needle, and so should its seam allowance.
c) Each colour is added to two sides of the block.
d) Alternate between light and dark strips to create the light and dark shading across the block.

Before joining blocks together for your quilt, lay them out to create your desired setting, so that you know exactly how each block will join the next one. It is very easy to pick up a block and turn it around before joining it, thereby throwing the overall design right out! Make up the eight rows of six blocks, then join rows together, butting together seams wherever possible.

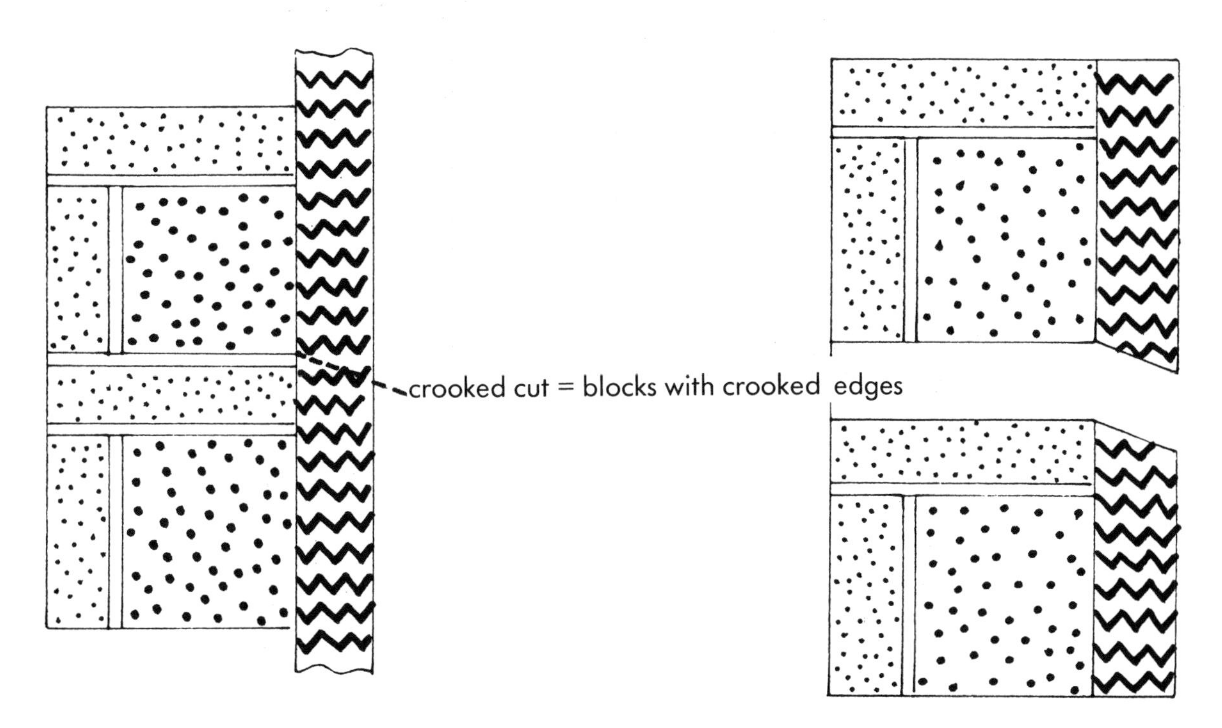

Figure 4.7

LOG CABIN —
BEING CREATIVE WITH THE BASIC METHOD

The method described for piecing Log Cabin blocks has generally been used to produce only quilts which consist of identical blocks throughout. (See plates 8 + 9)

While these are very attractive, they are not the limit of the possibilities for speed piecing Log Cabin. The principle of the 'washing line' method is to be *adding the same fabric* to a large number of blocks at one time. Whether or not the blocks to which you are adding the fabric are identical is not important.

Thus you could be adding the same strip of navy blue to a selection of blocks with different coloured centres, or blocks in various stages of completion. (Figure 4.8). This method has been used to create the picture quilt in plate 11.

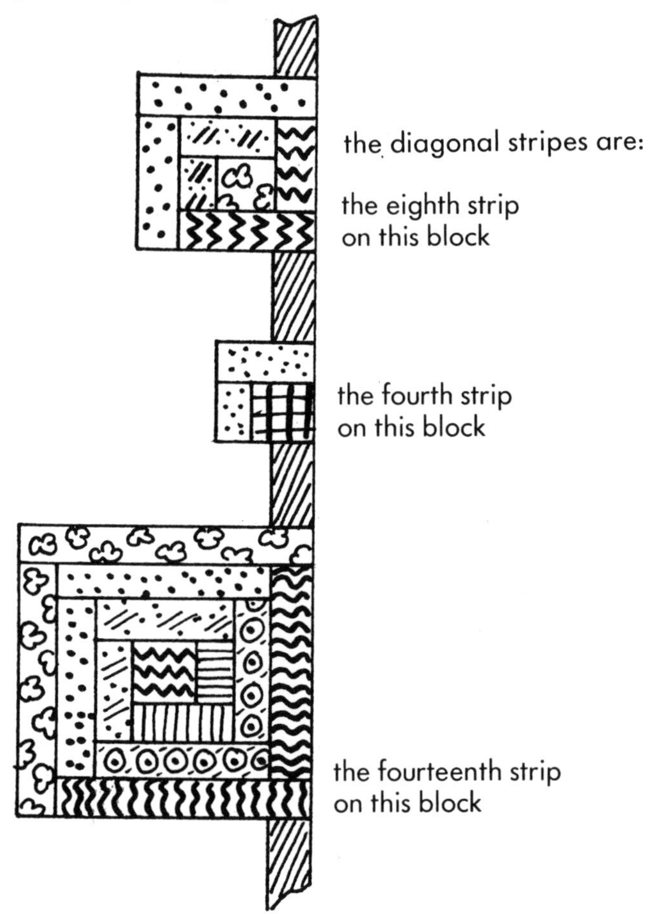

Figure 4.8

Naturally this takes a little more planning in the design stage. For a picture Log Cabin quilt it would be necessary to draw up an initial plan of the quilt to determine colour layout. For example, a layout for the quilt in plate 11 may look like this. (Figure 4.9)

The plan shows blocks pieced primarily in dark blue (sea), light blue (sky) and brown (sand), though few of these are identical, and in addition there are a few individually pieced blocks for the sun and the boats.

This quilt uses a total of 26 fabrics. Some blocks are identical, but most are variations on a colour theme. Apart from the few specific blocks mentioned above, the quilter was able to piece at least 4-6 blocks at a time.

This method also enables the creation of a scrap-look Log Cabin quilt without the laborious piecing of one block at a time. The fabric quantities at the beginning of this chapter could be used as a guide, but using a large number of fabrics divided into lights, darks and centres. Cut the same total number of strips (47 light, 54 dark, 4 centres) then begin piecing in a random sequence while still adding a single fabric to several blocks at once, only ensuring that you alternate between light and dark on opposite sides of the block.

Figure 4.9

clouds	clouds	clouds	sun	sun
sky / clouds	sky	sky	sky	sky
boat / water	water	water	boat / water	water
water	water	boat / water	water	water
water	water	water	water	water
boat / water	water	water	water	boat / water
sand / water	sand / water	sand / water	sand / water	sand / water
sand / rocks	sand / rocks	sand / rocks	sand / rocks	sand / rocks

A further possibility is the 'curved' log cabin. This is achieved by cutting all the strips on one side (e.g. all the lights) half the finished width (plus seam allowance) of the other side. Centres should be cut the wider width.

So a block with centres and dark fabrics cut 2 inches wide (1½ inches finished) and lights cut 1½ inches wide (¾ inch finished) would look like this. (Figure 4.10)

Using the standard three fabrics on each side, this block would end up being 1½ inch/3.75 cm smaller in each direction than the blocks used in the example quilt. However, by adding either two more light strips or one more dark, this block would be brought up to the finished size of the standard Log Cabin blocks used in this chapter. This 'curved' Log Cabin could add an extra dimension of design possibilities to quilts like the picture quilt in plate 11.

Yet another variation is to use only one fabric for all the strips on one side of the block, while still using a variety on the other. Some of the Amish quilts use this to great effect, with black on one side of the block and bright solid colours on the other. The colours appear to 'float' and rise up out of the black.

Log Cabin is one of the most versatile of quilt blocks, and whole books have been devoted to design possibilities. Most can make use of speed piecing techniques to at least some extent.

the diagonal break-up between light and dark appears to curve on this block

Figure 4.10

ALTERING THE SIZE OF YOUR LOG CABIN QUILT

Most of the methods for altering the size of the quilt have already been touched upon.

The blocks themselves can be altered in size by either:

(i) changing the width of the strips, or

(ii) changing the number of strips in each block

Thus for a cot quilt you may wish to cut all the strips of fabric 1¼ inch wide instead of the 1¾ inch and 2¾ inch strips used in the example quilt. This would make 5¼ inch/13.5 cm blocks which would allow all the setting possibilities of a full-sized quilt on a small scale.

Similarly, for a queen-sized quilt you may decide to increase the size of the blocks by introducing additional fabrics, adding a fourth and fifth light and dark strip to each block.

The most obvious way to alter the size of the quilt is to change the number of blocks you make. Just be sure to keep in mind that some settings of Log Cabin require an even number of blocks in each direction to work. Thus the Barn Raising setting could not be increased by one block in either direction or it would be thrown off centre — so instead of 48 blocks (six across, eight down) you would have to make 64 (8 x 8) or 80 (8 x 10) blocks. Other settings, such as Straight Furrows, do not require an even number of blocks, and can be increased by one block in either direction (56 blocks — 7 x 8, 63 blocks — 7 x 9, etc.).

As with any quilt, the size can be altered quite considerably by the border. Log Cabin lends itself admirably to the re-introduction of any number of the fabrics from the quilt into the border — see Chapter 6.

Figure 5.1 Amish Basket Quilt

CHAPTER 5

AMISH BASKET QUILT

The Amish Basket quilt dealt with in this chapter is based on the Rapid Triangle Method, which is a quick way of joining pairs of half-square triangles (◪). Again, as with the 'washing line' method for Log Cabin blocks, I can claim no originality for this method. It has been around for a long time, and appears in numerous books, but nowhere have I seen it attributed to one particular person.

The Rapid Triangle Method is very versatile, as half-square triangles are used in a wide variety of quilt blocks. Additional possibilities and variations will be discussed at the end of the chapter.

The basket block described in this chapter can be constructed in either of two ways. (Figure 5.2)

To keep it simple, all instructions will show Basket 1. The triangles can just as easily be made into Basket 2, or into more complex basket blocks.

To begin with, I will describe the general instructions for the Rapid Triangle Method.

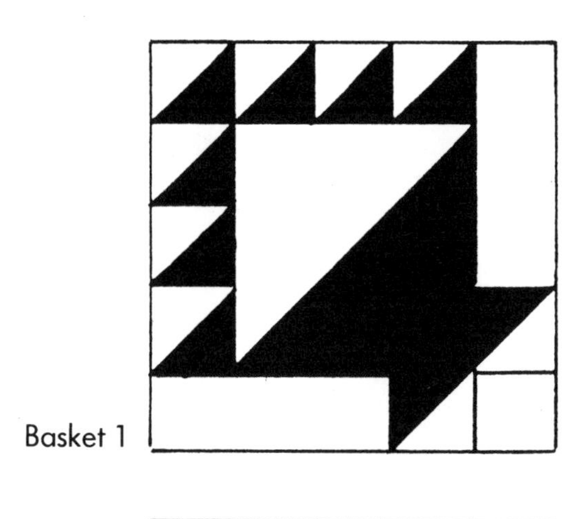

Basket 2

Figure 5.2

THE RAPID TRIANGLE METHOD

Place two fabrics right sides together. Have on top the fabric that will most easily show pencil/tailor's chalk markings.

Draw up squares on the top fabric (Figure 5.3). The size of the squares is determined by the size of the finished triangles required.

Draw diagonal lines through the squares (a). Stitch through the squares on either side of the diagonals (b), using the width of the pressure foot as a seam guide. Avoid sewing through the tips of adjoining squares (c).

squares drawn up onto top of fabric

(a) diagonals drawn through squares

(b) stitch through squares on either side of diagonals

(c) avoid sewing through tips of adjoining squares

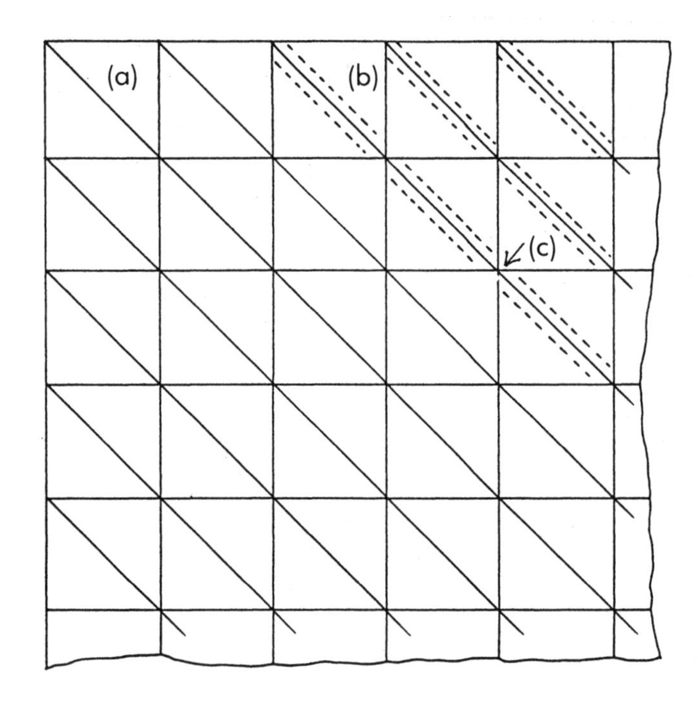

Figure 5.3

Cut out squares, then through the diagonal line, and open out pairs of triangles. (Figure 5.4)

Figure 5.4

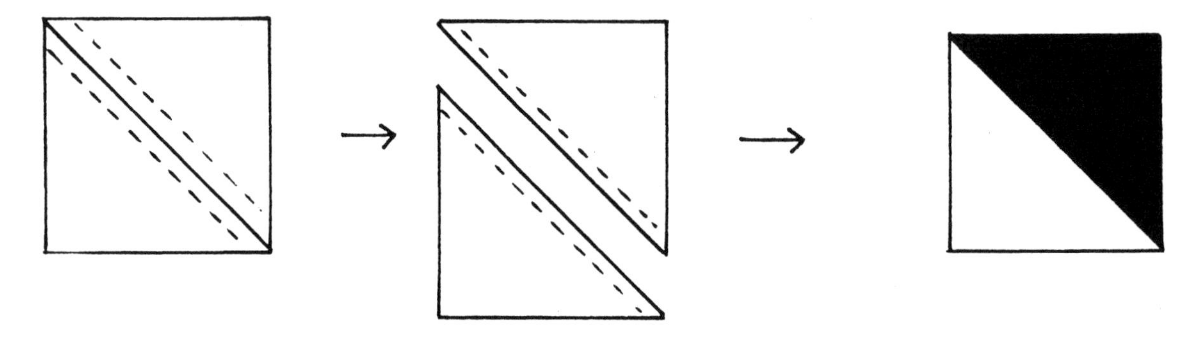

REQUIREMENTS

Double Bed Quilt

20 blocks (4 x 5 blocks) measuring:
(without borders) 148 cm x 185 cm
(58 inches x 73 inches)

(with 25 cm borders) 198 cm x 235 cm
(78 inches x 92 inches)

Queen Bed Quilt

30 blocks (5 x 6 blocks) measuring:
(without borders) 185 cm x 222 cm
(73 inches x 88 inches)

(with 25 cm borders) 235 cm x 272 cm
(92 inches x 107 inches)

20-Block Quilt

Fabric 1 (the basket) — 1.1 m (1¼ yds)

Fabric 2 (background to basket) — 1.7 m (1⅞ yds)

Fabric 3 (unpieced blocks) — 2.2 m (2½ yds)

or borders up to 25 cm (10 inches)
wide, with mitred corners — 2.5 m (2¾ yds)

30-Block Quilt

Fabric 1 (the basket) — 1.5 m (1⅝ yds)

Fabric 2 (background to basket) — 2.4 m (2⅝ yds)

Fabric 3 (unpieced blocks) — 3.5 m (3⅞ yds)

Border Fabric — for borders up to 25 cm (10 inches)
wide, with mitred corners — 2.8 m (3⅛ yds)

The unpieced blocks may be made from the same fabric as the background to the baskets (plates 17 + 20). This will cause the baskets to stand out boldly from a uniform background. If this is to be the case, simply add together the two fabric requirements, Fabric 2 and Fabric 3.

METHOD

Each block consists of:

- 9 pairs Rapid Triangles — small
- 1 pair Rapid Triangles — large
- 2 strips (side)
- 1 square (base)

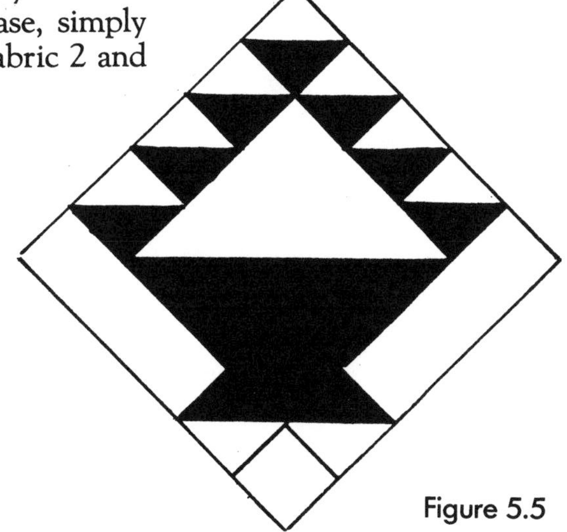

Figure 5.5

Figure 5.6

Figure 5.8

Figure 5.9

Figure 5.10

Figure 5.11

Step 1 — *Draw up grids of squares according to the Rapid Triangle method*

a) Small triangles — mark up 3 inch/7.7 cm squares.
For a 20-block quilt, grid must be 13 squares wide and 7 squares long.
For a 30-block quilt, grid must be 14 squares wide and 10 squares long.

b) Large triangles — mark up 7¼ inch/18.5 cm squares.
For a 20-block quilt, grid is 5 squares wide, 2 squares long.
For a 30-block quilt, grid is 5 squares wide, 3 squares long.

c) Side strips and squares — cut 2⅝ inch/6.7 cm strips across full width of Fabric 2. Cut eight strips for a 20-block quilt and 12 strips for a 30-block quilt. Cut these strips again to provide two 7 inch/17.8 cm lengths and one 2⅝ inch/6.7 cm square for each block.

Step 2 — Make up batches of paired triangles according to the Rapid Triangle method. You will need nine pairs of small triangles and one pair of large triangles per block. Iron the seam allowance on the small triangles towards Fabric 2 (the background fabric). Iron the seam allowance on large triangles towards Fabric 1 (basket fabric). This will minimise bulk when the blocks are made up. Cut side strips and squares as indicated above.

Step 3 — *Assembling the blocks*

Join three pairs of small triangles for the left-hand side of the block (note direction of both triangles and seam allowances). (Figure 5.6)

Join 4 pairs of small triangles for the right-hand side of the block (note direction of both triangles and seam allowances). (Figure 5.7)

Join the shorter group of paired triangles to the left-hand side of the large triangles (Figure 5.8). Iron seam allowance towards the large triangles.

Join the larger group of paired triangles to the right-hand side of the block, ensuring the points meet those of adjoining triangles. Iron seam allowance towards the large triangle. (Figure 5.9)

Join one pair of small triangles to each of the two 7 inch/17.8 cm strips of Fabric 2. Note the direction of both the triangles and the seams. (Figure 5.10)

Add the single square to strip No. 2. (Figure 5.11)

Add strip No. 1 above to the left-hand side of the block. (Figure 5.12)

Add strip No. 2, above, to the right-hand side of the block. (Figure 5.13)

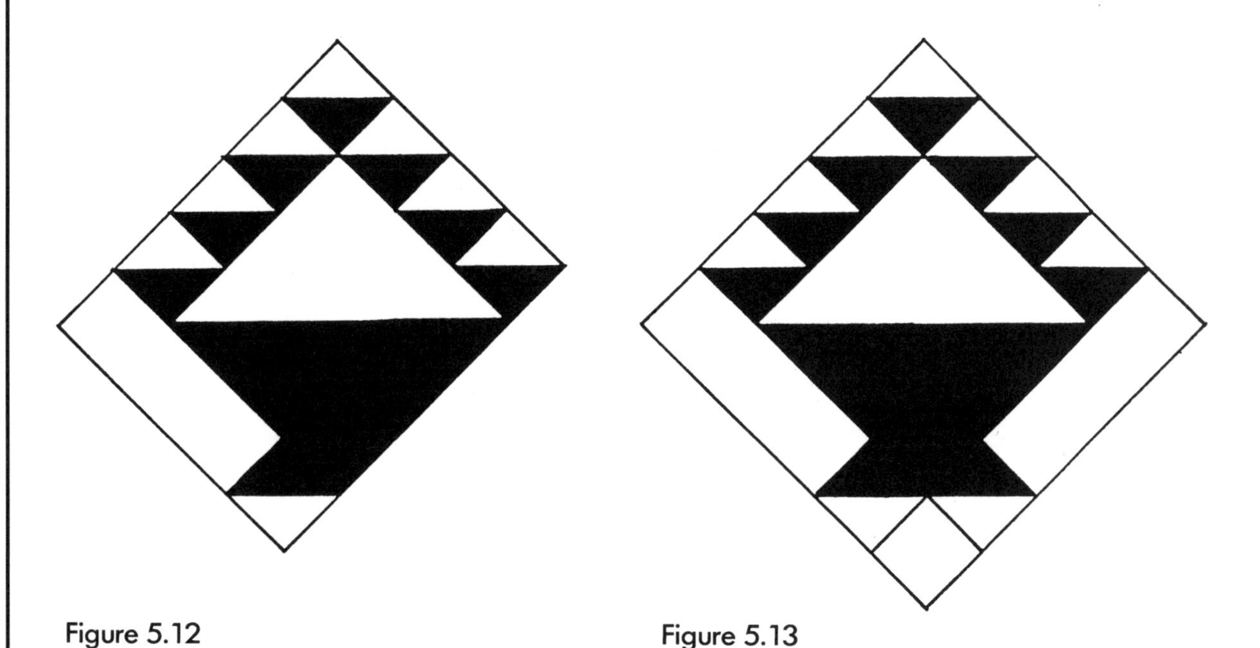

Figure 5.12

Figure 5.13

Step 4 — When you have made up all the basket blocks, measure them. They should all measure the same — if not, take an average. Generally speaking, a difference of about 0.5 cm (¼ inch) can be eased in or stretched to fit the next block (this is not an ideal situation, but at this stage, 'fudging' usually beats remaking!). If you have used polyester or poly-cotton in your blocks, they will have considerably less 'give'. So while all cotton blocks might vary, say, between 10 inches/25.5 cm and 10½ inches/26.5 cm, blocks containing polyester should not have an overall variation of more than about 5 mm (¼ inch) (requiring only 2.5 mm (⅛ inch) easing or stretching). Any greater variance will require the trimming of the blocks. This should be done so that the least damage is caused to the rows of small triangles at the top of the block, as it is here that the chopping off of points will be most noticeable.

After the blocks have been pressed, measured and, if necessary, trimmed, you will have to cut the plain (unpieced) blocks from Fabric 3. These will be cut to the average measurements of the basket blocks. You will need:

for a 20-block quilt — 12 unpieced blocks

for a 30-block quilt — 20 unpieced blocks

As the blocks are all set on point, you will have to join basket blocks with alternate plain squares to form diagonal strips of quilt (unlike the Double Irish Chain or Log Cabin, where rows were joined horizontally). Each row will have to be finished with a half-square triangle in Fabric 3. The size of these triangles can be estimated quite easily.

CUTTING THE HALF-SQUARE TRIANGLES

Cut squares from Fabric 3 that measure *1 cm (⅜ inch) more* in each direction than your average basket block. Cut this in two diagonally. This will yield two half-square triangles. (Figure 5.14)

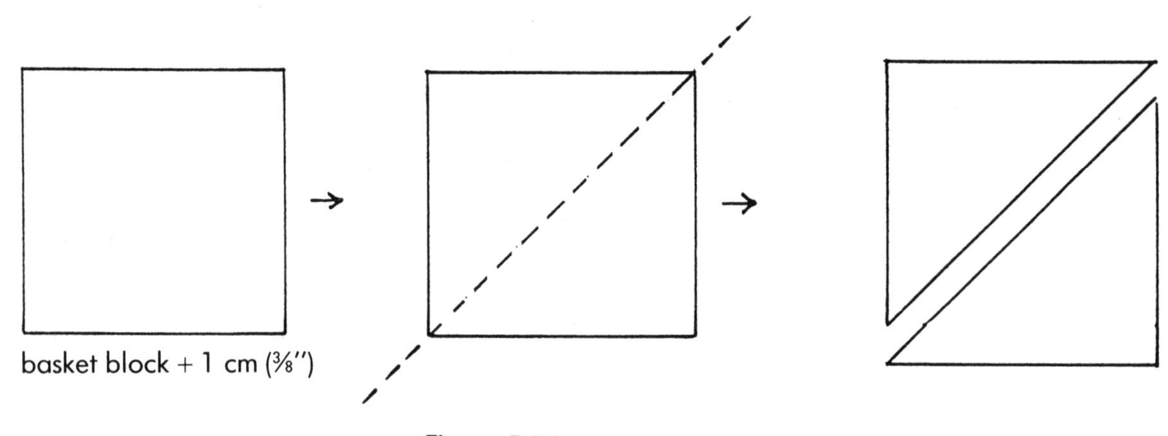

Figure 5.14

Remember two things when joining these triangles to the last block in the row.

i) the triangle is joined so that the bias edge forms the outside edge of the quilt

ii) when a triangle is joined to a square, the point of the triangle will always stick out past the end of the square (it is the intersections of seam allowances that must meet)

Once all the blocks are assembled into rows, press all the seam allowances towards the plain (unpieced) blocks. This will ensure that seams butt together along each row.

Join the diagonal rows to form the quilt top. You will now require only four small triangles to fill the corners of the quilt. (Figure 5.15)

Figure 5.15

CUTTING THE FOUR CORNER TRIANGLES

Cut a square from Fabric 3 that measures *2 cm (¾ inch) more* in each direction than your average basket block. Cut this diagonally both ways to form four triangles (Figure 5.16). Add these to the corners of the quilt top.

You are now ready to add the border. Remember when handling this quilt that all the outer edges are on the bias, and can be easily stretched. When measuring for borders, do not measure right on the edge of the fabric, stretching it as you go. Measure *a few centimetres (inches) in* from the edge, with the quilt top flat on the ground and neither wrinkled nor stretched.

Figure 5.16

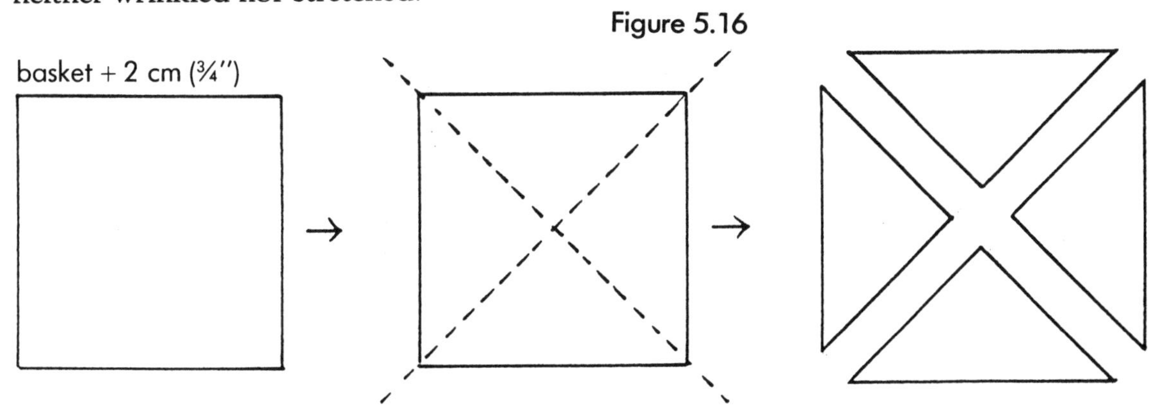

VARIATIONS OF THE EXAMPLE QUILT

The basket blocks in the example quilt are set 'on point'. The reason for this is not only an aesthetic one, sitting the baskets upright. Setting the baskets 'on point' means you need to piece less baskets, as the blocks set on point will measure approximately 36 cm (14¼ inches) across as opposed to 26 cm (10¼ inches) if set on square. (Figure 5.17)

Figure 5.17

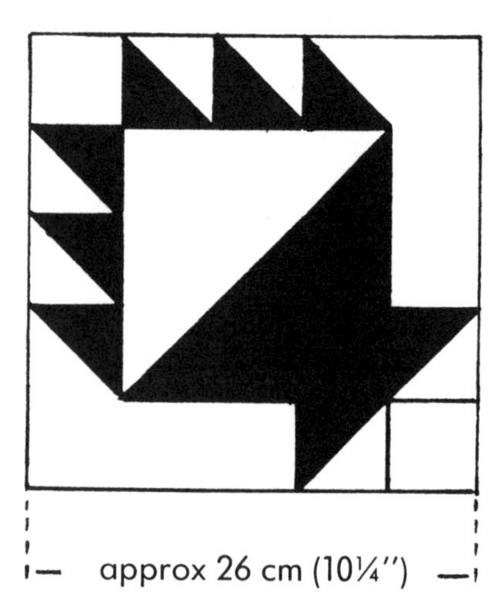

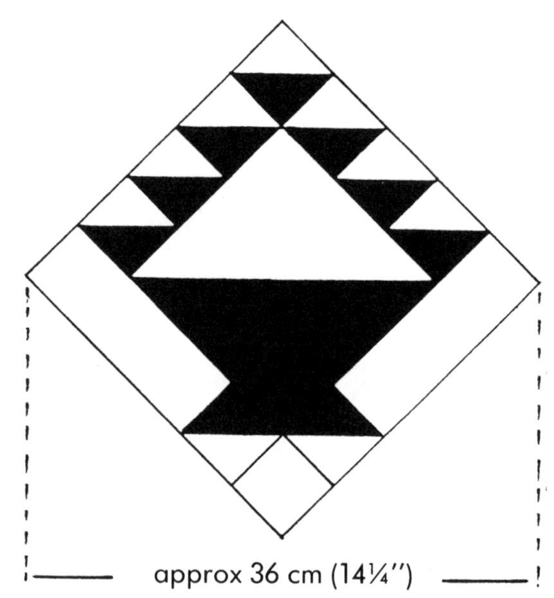

However, adding the unpieced blocks in between the baskets virtually demands that you fill the space with lots of hand quilting. If hand quilting is not your forte, there are a couple of other settings for the basket blocks you may wish to try.

The unpieced blocks could be replaced with more basket blocks, perhaps in a different colour combination, or using the second style of basket shown on page 73. (Figure 5.18)

Figure 5.18

This could be further expanded by adding sashing between the blocks. (Figure 5.19)
Alternatively, you may prefer to set all the blocks square rather than on point, with sashing strips in between. This is a good way to introduce additional colour to the quilt. (Figure 5.20). Additional colours can also be introduced in the border (see plates 17 + 20).

Figure 5.19

Figure 5.20

A traditional Amish quilt would have half the basket blocks facing one end of the quilt and half facing the other. This means the quilt has no 'top' or 'bottom' and can be turned round on the bed to ensure even wear (see plate 18).

The size of the basket blocks depends totally on the size of the grid used for drawing up the Rapid Triangles. The example quilt used 3 inch squares for the small triangles. The resultant pairs of triangles created $2\frac{5}{16}$ inch squares (excluding seam allowance) and therefore the finished block size was $11\frac{1}{2}$ inch. A $2\frac{1}{2}$ inch grid would produce a $8\frac{3}{4}$ inch block while a $3\frac{1}{2}$ inch grid would produce a $14\frac{3}{8}$ inch block. Remember that the size of the large triangles would also need to be adjusted.
would also need to be adjusted.

Having mastered the Rapid Triangle method on this Basket Quilt, try utilising it on other traditional quilt designs. Pinwheels, Ocean Waves and Feathered Stars are just a few of the many designs that can be made more simply by piecing the paired triangles in this way. (Figure 5.21)

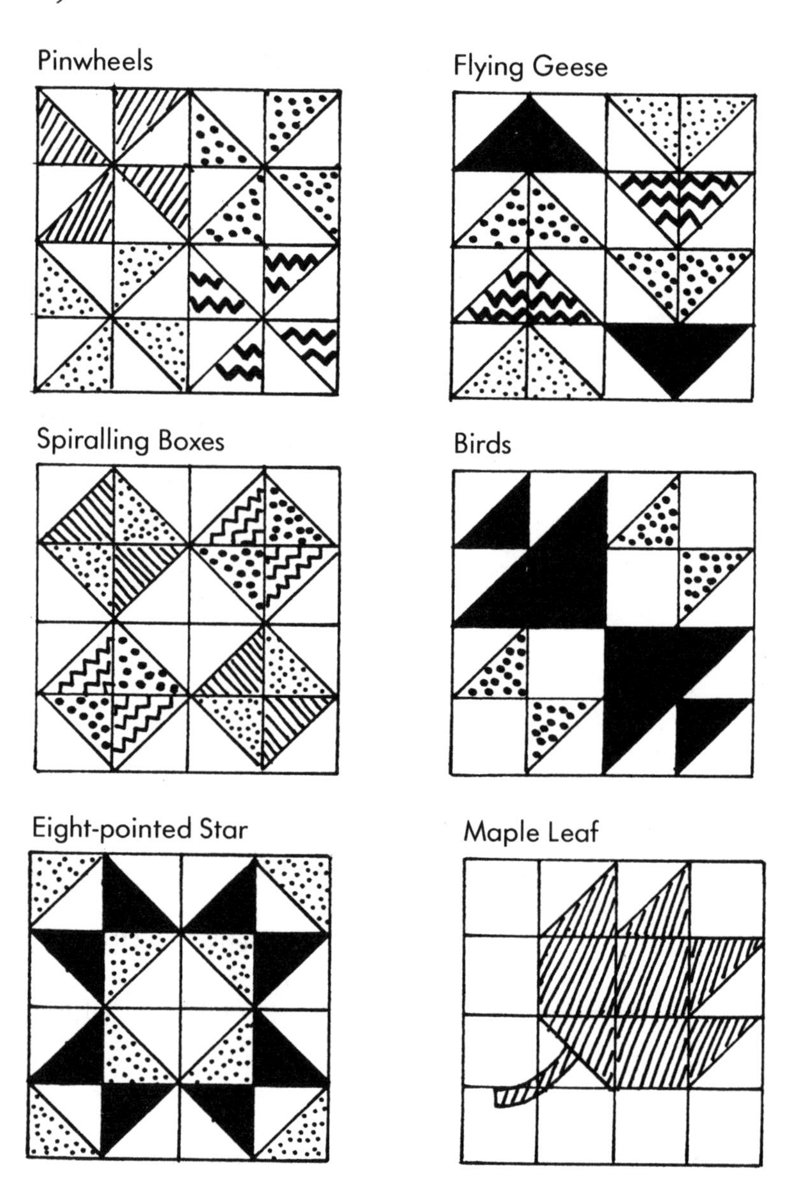

Figure 5.21

CHAPTER 6

BORDERS

The border of a quilt, like the frame of a picture, can be anything from very simple to very ornate, utterly traditional to totally abstract. Either way, it can do a great deal to enhance and extend the quilt design. Borders should be regarded as an integral part of the overall quilt design, well thought out, not added almost as an afterthought just to get the quilt finished or make it bigger!

The quilts in this book are very traditional designs, and most of those illustrated have very simple, plain borders, but there is no need to limit yourself — a border may be every bit as creative as the quilt design itself, and, as such, will add an extra dimension to the quilt. Consider the border of the Loan Star quilt in plate 16. This is by no means a standard one-colour border, yet its construction is simple and it enhances and extends the design features of the star.

At the end of this chapter I have illustrated a few border variations. These are designed just to get you thinking — the possibilities are endless, and whole books have been written on the subject of quilt settings and borders. (Jan T. Urquhart, *Designing Quilts is Fun*, Mondo Publications, 1990; Jinny Beyer, *The Quilter's Album of Blocks and Borders*, EPM Publications).

Fabric for borders is usually cut down the length of the fabric. There are two reasons for this —

i) The full border can be cut from a length of fabric without requiring joins.
ii) The lengthwise grain (warp) of a fabric is always firmer, with less stretch than the cross-grain (weft). This creates a strong stable frame for the quilt.

Most fabrics today measure between 110 cm (43 inches) and 120 cm (47 inches) wide, so it is possible to cut four borders up to 27 cm (11 inches) wide from a width of fabric (after first removing the selvedges). Wider borders will require twice the length of fabric.

SIMPLE BORDERS

Simple borders using just one fabric can be put on the quilt in two ways:

a) straight cut borders, or
b) mitred borders.

Before adding borders, check the finished dimensions of the quilt centre. Opposite sides *should* measure the same. If there is a variation, an average measurement should be taken, and borders calculated around this measurement. This step is very important to ensure the quilt finishes a perfect square or rectangle, and hangs well.

STRAIGHT CUT BORDERS

Cut two side borders the required width down the border fabric. Cut to the exact length of the quilt sides (or the average measurement mentioned above). Sew these onto the long sides of the quilt first. (Figure 6.1)

When the side borders are on, measure across the top and bottom of the quilt. Cut two more borders to this length and sew on across the top and bottom of the quilt. (Figure 6.2)

If a second border is required, simply repeat the process, adding side borders first, then top and bottom. Variations on this simple border are illustrated later in this chapter.

A point to note when measuring your quilt top is to take the measurement slightly in from the edge, not right on it. There is always a danger that the outside edge will be distorted when measuring — that bias edges will stretch, and seam ends will open out — giving an incorrect measurement. Move your tape measure a few centimetres in from the edge then measure down the quilt.

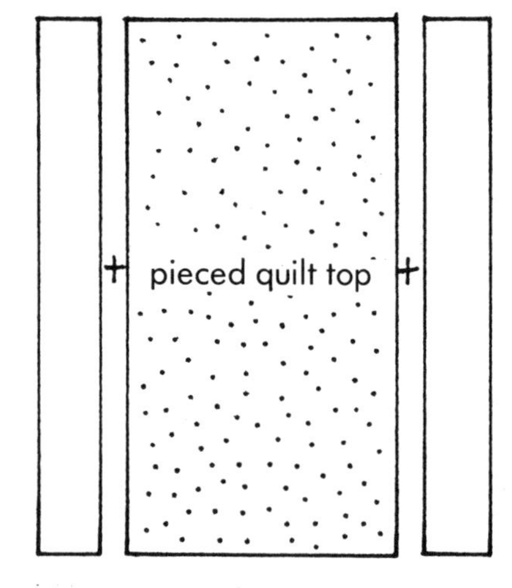

Figure 6.1

Figure 6.2

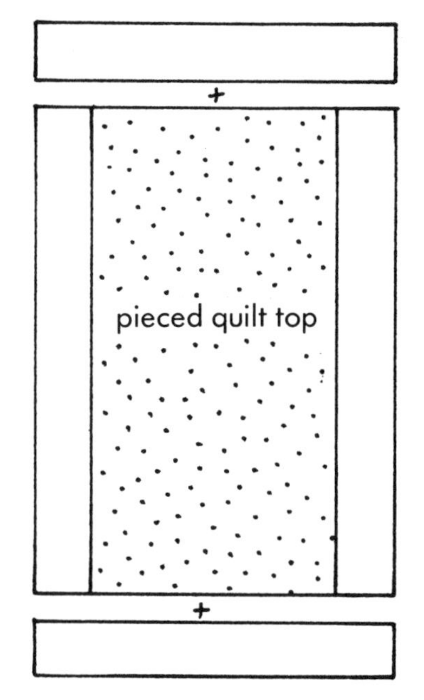

MITRED BORDERS

Border strips for mitred borders will measure the length of the side to be bordered + twice the border width + an overlap of 2-3 cm (about 1 inch). (This is to make the intersection of the borders clearly visible — see Figure 6.3, below.)

Pin the borders to the quilt, matching centres first then working out to the sides. You should have the same sized overhang at each end of every border. Sew the borders to all sides of the quilt top with a ¼ inch/6 mm seam allowance, *beginning and ending at the seam line,* not at the outer edge of the quilt. Tie off ends of thread.

Lay the whole quilt out as flat as possible, wrong side up. Now place one border flat over the other at one corner (Figure 6.3) and draw a line from A to B as indicated. Reverse the two borders so that the bottom one is now on top, and again draw a line from A to B on this one. Pick up the quilt, and with fabrics right sides together, match the two pencil lines together and sew through them. Cut away excess seam allowance. Press the seam and repeat the process at the other three corners.

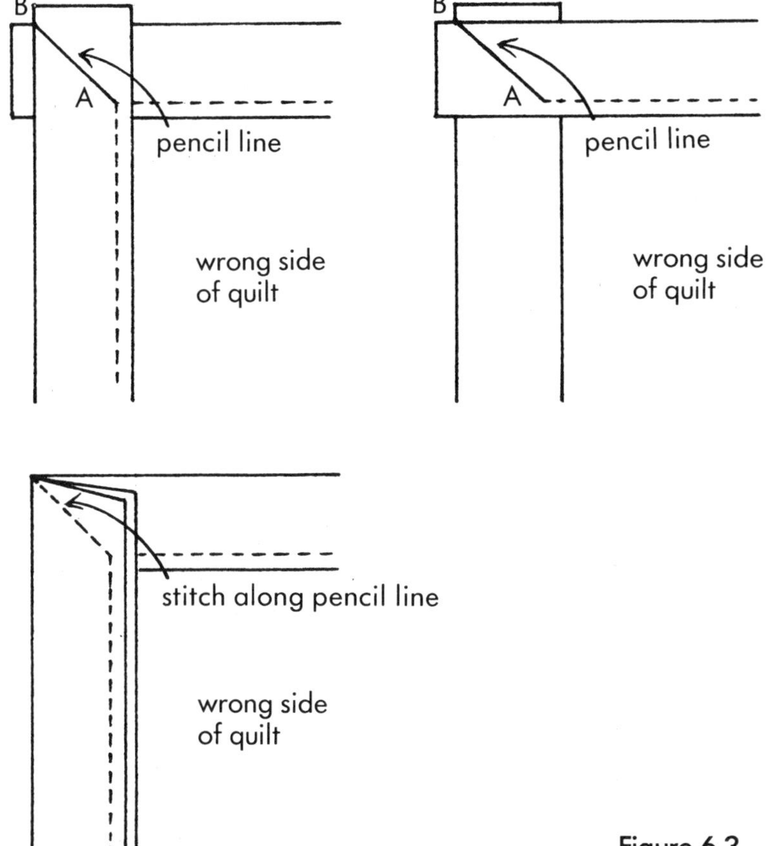

Figure 6.3

If you are adding a series of borders which are to be mitred, join all the border strips together first for each side of the quilt, and sew on as if it were a single border. Remember to match up all the different border strips where they meet on the mitred seam. Also ensure that each set of border strips is long enough to make the full outside edge of the quilt. (Figure 6.4)

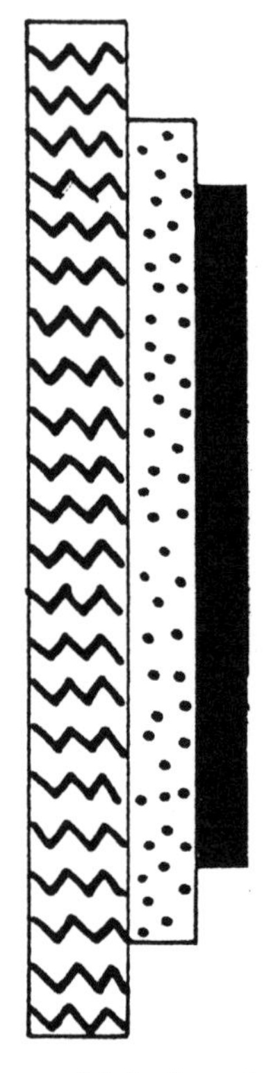

multiple border strips
joined to form single border

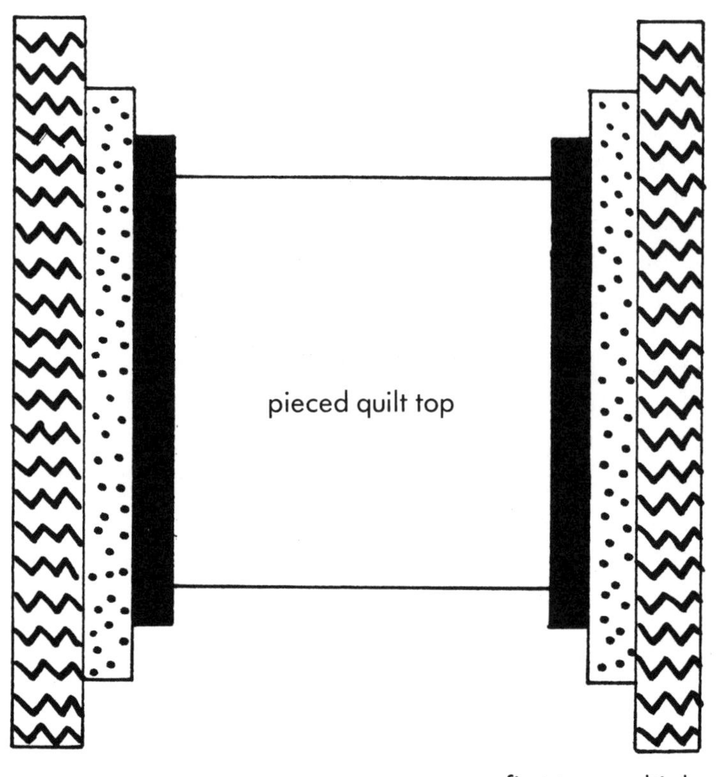

first two multiple
borders added

successive border strips meet
up neatly at mitred seam

Figure 6.4

SOME INTERESTING BORDER VARIATIONS

Variation 1 — Straight-cut borders with setting squares.

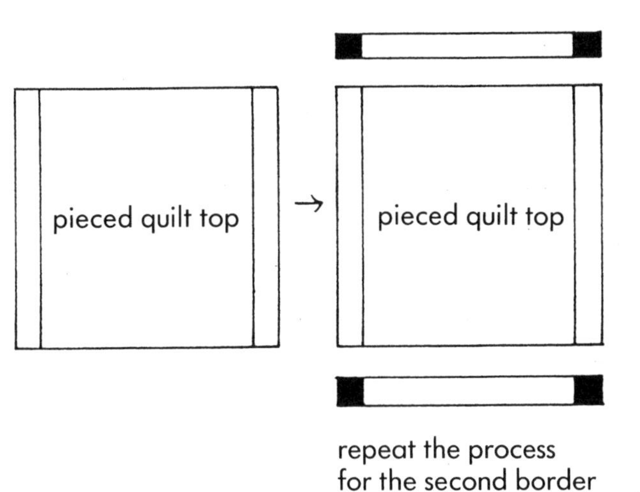

Figure 6.5

Variation 2 — Multiple borders can include the off-cuts from strip piecing (this is used in the Lone Star illustration).

Figure 6.6

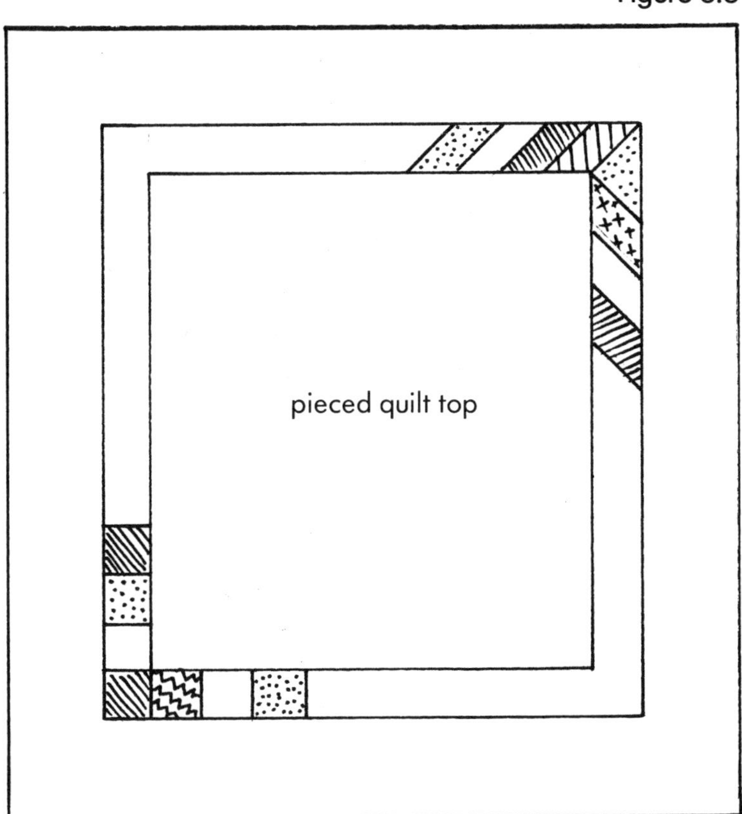

Variation 3 — Random inserts of contrast add drama to a border, and also solve a problem when a single full length of fabric is unavailable for the border. See a similar example in plate 16.

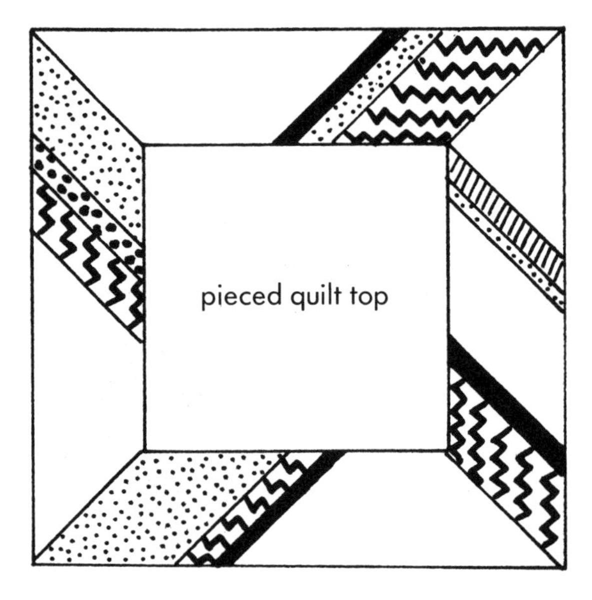

Figure 6.7

Variation 4 — The Rapid Triangle method can be used to make a sawtooth border between the quilt centre and the outer border.

Figure 6.8

Variation 5 — Strip pieced borders can be joined to Nine-patch corner blocks to give the impression of being woven. Five strips will give an even more complex border.

Figure 6.9

Variation 6

Figure 6.10

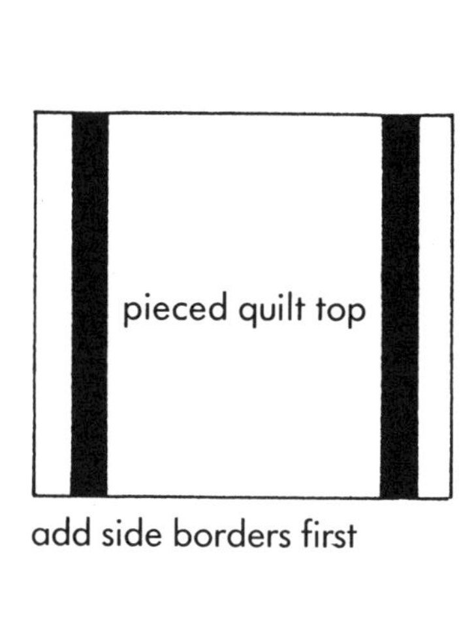

add side borders first

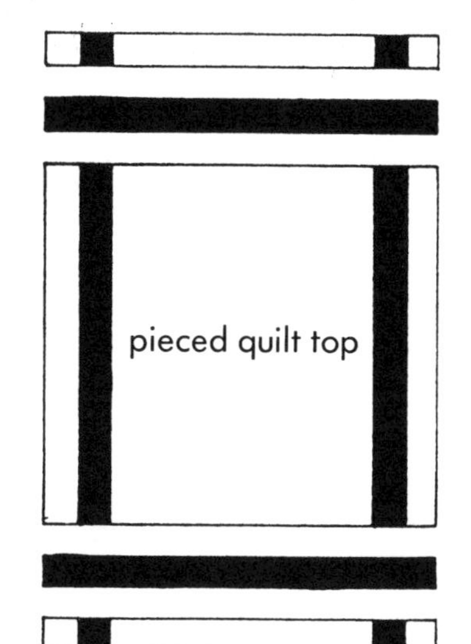

=

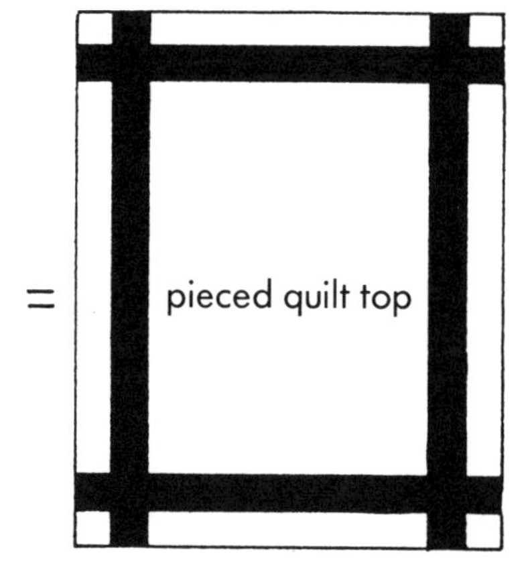

Variation 7 — Simple Seminole piecing is also effective in a border.

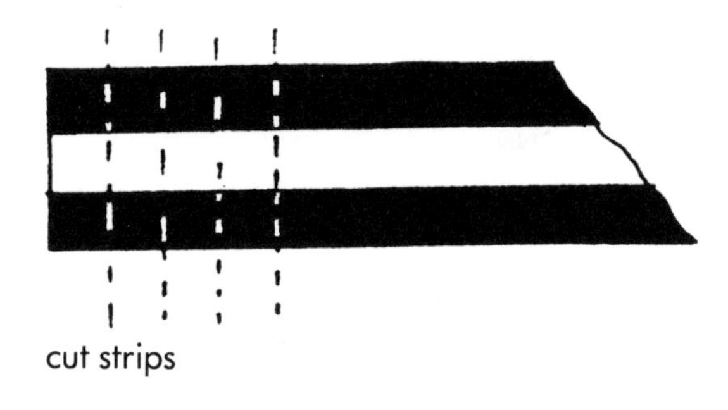

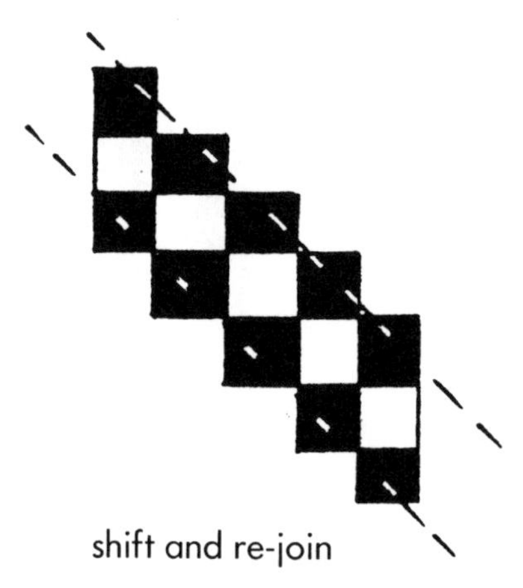

remember to leave a
seam allowance when
trimming seminole strips

Figure 6.11

CHAPTER 7

PUTTING IT ALL TOGETHER

Once you have completed your quilt top you will be ready to put your quilt together. While it is not the purpose of this book to go into details past the piecing of the patchwork top, I will outline roughly what is involved in finishing the quilt. I must emphasise this is not a detailed account of the processes involved — more information can be found in books dealing specifically with quilting, e.g. Diane Leone's *Fine Hand Quilting* (Leone Publ. 1986) and *Heirloom Machine Quilting* by Harriet Hargreave (C&T Publishing).

There is a saying that 'a quilt is not a quilt until it's quilted'. A quilt is a 'sandwich' of three layers — the back, the batting (wadding) which provides the warmth, and the pieced top. These three layers must be held together in one of three ways to make the quilt functional. The three ways are tying, machine quilting and hand quilting.

Whichever way is chosen to finish the quilt, some basic preparation must be done first.

PREPARATION FOR QUILTING

Put together the fabric for the back of the quilt (you will probably have to join pieces). The back should be about 5 cm (2 inches) bigger all round than your quilt top. Lay the back out, wrong side up, on a wooden or cork floor (carpet can become a nuisance, as will become clear). Smooth out the wrinkles, and tape the edges to the floor at intervals with masking tape (this will prevent it buckling up).

How you proceed from this point will depend on the type of quilting you intend to do. As a rough generalisation it can be said that the visual effect of the three quilting methods is proportional to the time they take. Let's look at them one at a time.

TYPES OF QUILTING

TYING

This is exactly what it sounds like — tying a thread through the three layers at regular intervals to hold them together. The effect on the quilt is to make it quite puffy — a bit like the studded backs on old fashioned lounge suites. Tying does not contribute much in terms of enhancing the quilt's overall design, and for this reason I feel it is best applied to a quilt top with a fairly 'busy' and regular overall design — e.g. Trip Around the World and Log Cabin.

The big advantage of tying a quilt is that it is very quick — a small quilt can be completed in an evening. However, it is not as strong as other methods, and rough treatment may result in the occasional tie coming loose.

How to tie a quilt

Prepare the three layers as mentioned above. Place a pin through all three layers at the points where you wish to tie. A regular pattern is recommended, e.g. around every four squares for Trip Around the World, or around the centres and at the intersections of Log Cabin blocks (Figure 7.1). Once the pins are in, the masking tape can be removed and the quilt lifted.

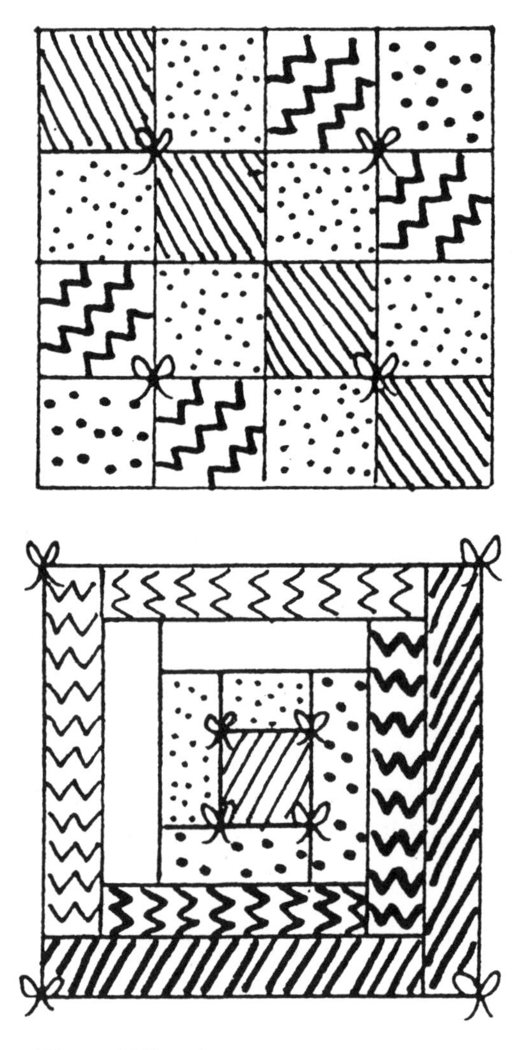

Figure 7.1

Tying can be done from the front or the back of the quilt. If from the front, use embroidery thread, pearl crochet cotton or 3 mm (1/8 inch) silk ribbon. If tying from the back, use quilting thread. One at a time, remove a pin, and take a stitch through all the layers with the thread/ribbon, then take another stitch in the same place and tie off with a double knot. (Figure 7.2). Embroidery threads or ribbon can be left as a tassle or tied in a bow. Quilting thread should be left long enough to be fed back into the batting with a needle. Continue until all pins have been replaced with ties.

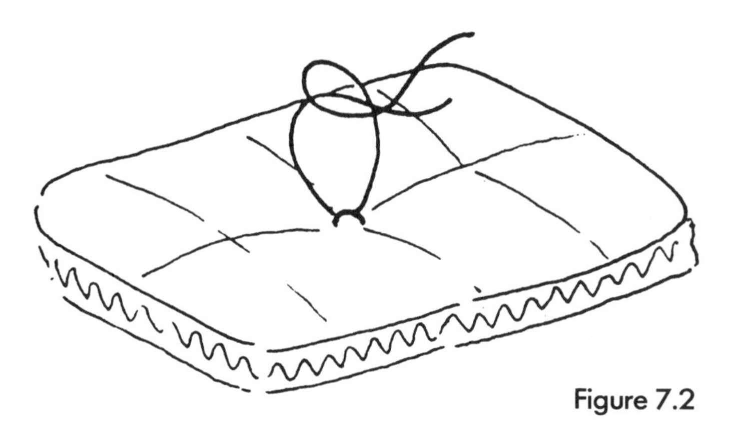

Figure 7.2

MACHINE QUILTING

If you are considering machine quilting it is worth investing in a book which deals with the subject in detail. Intricate designs can be done by machine, but these require considerable practice, and are not for the beginner. A more basic method of machine quilting is to follow the piecing lines, quilting 'in the ditch' next to the seams.

Machine quilting is much faster than hand quilting, and much stronger than tying. It will also add a degree of visual interest to the surface of the quilt, depending on where you machine and how adept you are at directing it. The big disadvantage of machine quilting is the sheer bulk of quilt that has to be manoeuvred through the arm of the sewing machine. A cot quilt is quite manageable. A Queen bed quilt can be a nightmare.

Any machine quilting is simpler with a walking foot on your machine. This is not a standard attachment, and prices vary enormously according to the brand of sewing machine. A walking foot acts like a dual feed, moving all the layers of the quilt through evenly. This avoids the problem of the pressure foot pushing one way and the feed dogs pulling the other (the problem you often encounter when sewing velvets and corduroys).

Prepare the layers as mentioned above, then pin them together with small safety pins at regular intervals, not more than about 10 cm (4 inches) apart, and placed away from the intended stitching lines (to avoid the pins going under the pressure foot).

Match the upper thread to your quilt top and the lower thread to the back, and use a medium-length stitch.

HAND QUILTING

Hand quilting gives by far the greatest visual interest to a quilt. It is not as tight as machine quilting, and therefore creates a soft shadow of design across the quilt. It is easy to change direction, so curves, feathers or flowers are easily done.

It also takes *much* longer than tying or machine quilting. While this can be a disadvantage to some, for most patchwork enthusiasts who are 'hooked' on hand quilting, it provides a peaceful and relaxing pastime.

Designs for hand quilting can be marked onto the quilt top before the layers are prepared, using either a fine lead pencil or quilter's carbon paper (Clover or Neweys are easiest to remove later). Designs can also be put on after the layers have been basted together (see below) by using a template and chalk pencil or following along the edges of masking tape (for straight lines).

Prepare the three layers as mentioned above. The layers must now be basted (tacked) together using a long needle and ordinary sewing thread.

Begin with a thread *longer than the entire length of the quilt.* Thread one end, and beginning at the centre of the quilt, baste out to the centre of one short side. Rethread the loose end of thread at the centre of the quilt and baste down to the other short side (Figure 7.3). If you can persuade a friend to help you, you can work together, with a needle at each end of the basting thread and each of you working out in the opposite direction. Never put a knot in the basting thread. You will end up with a bulge in that part of the quilt.

Figure 7.3

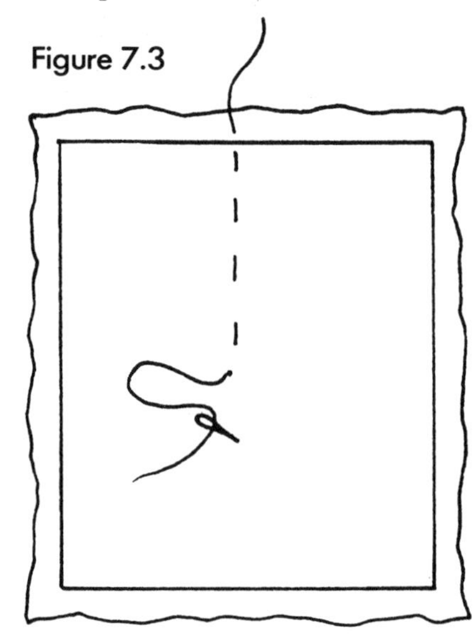

Do the same across the quilt, then diagonally to the corners. Now fill in wedges of basting in each of these triangular sections, always working from the centre of the quilt out to the sides. (Figure 7.4) (See also plate 22)

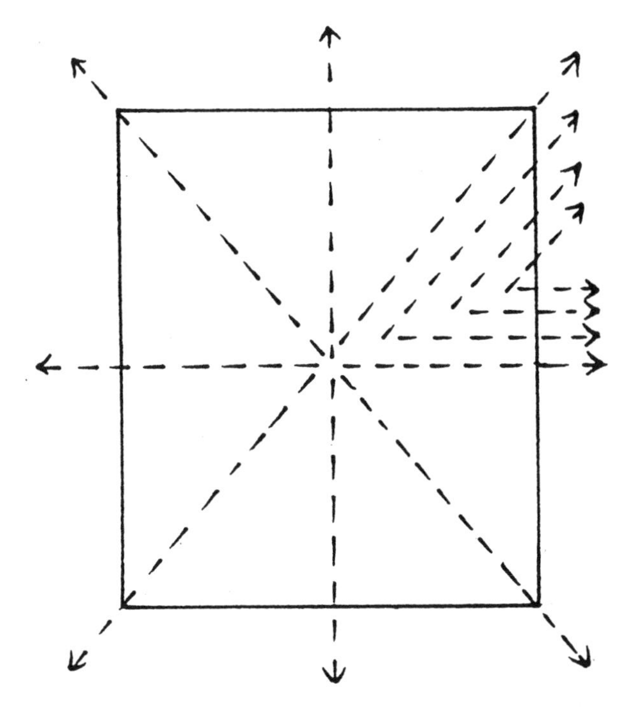

Figure 7.4

How to hand quilt

For hand quilting you will need a quilting hoop to hold the work firmly. Place the centre of the quilt over the bottom half of the hoop, smooth it out, and put the top of the hoop over it. Pat the centre a little to loosen it — it needn't be drum tight.

The quilting stitch is simply a running stitch, made with quilting thread and small needles called 'Betweens'. However, you will find it takes a little time before you can easily make short, even running stitches through the thickness of the three layers of the quilt.

Begin by tying a knot in the end of the quilting thread. Use short lengths of thread — about 45 cm (18 inches) to avoid tangling. Put the needle in about 2.5 cm (1 inch) from where you want to begin quilting and run it through the batting, bringing it up where the quilting is to start. Give a gentle tug so that the knot goes down into the quilt and lodges in the batting. Begin the running stitches, trying to put the needle in perpendicular to the fabric (this will keep the stitches short). Keep your other hand under the quilt, using the index or middle finger of this hand to feel the point of the needle coming through and redirect it up. You will soon discover that you need a thimble on the middle finger of the top hand, which is pushing the needle, and possibly on the finger below as well. As you push the needle from the top and redirect it up from the bottom, use your top thumb to make a ridge for the needle to go through. (Figure 7.5). You will soon find it is as easy to take several stitches at a time, rocking the needle up and down, as it is to take one.

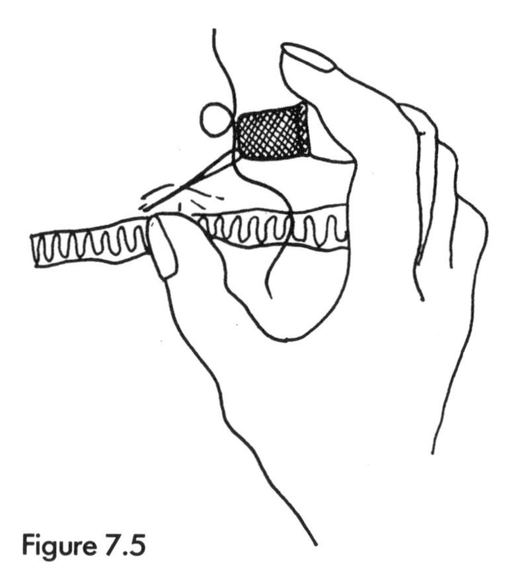

Figure 7.5

Where possible, avoid stitching through the extra thickness of seam allowances. If this is unavoidable, e.g. when crossing seam intersections, you may find you have to take the stitch in two sections, through to the back, then back up to the surface of the quilt.

To finish a line of quilting, either tie a knot before the last stitch and pop it through into the batting, as you did to begin, *or* take a small backstitch, *or* take the last stitch through to the back of the quilt then bring the needle back up to the surface, splitting the thread of the last stitch then feeding the end back into the batting. (Figure 7.6)

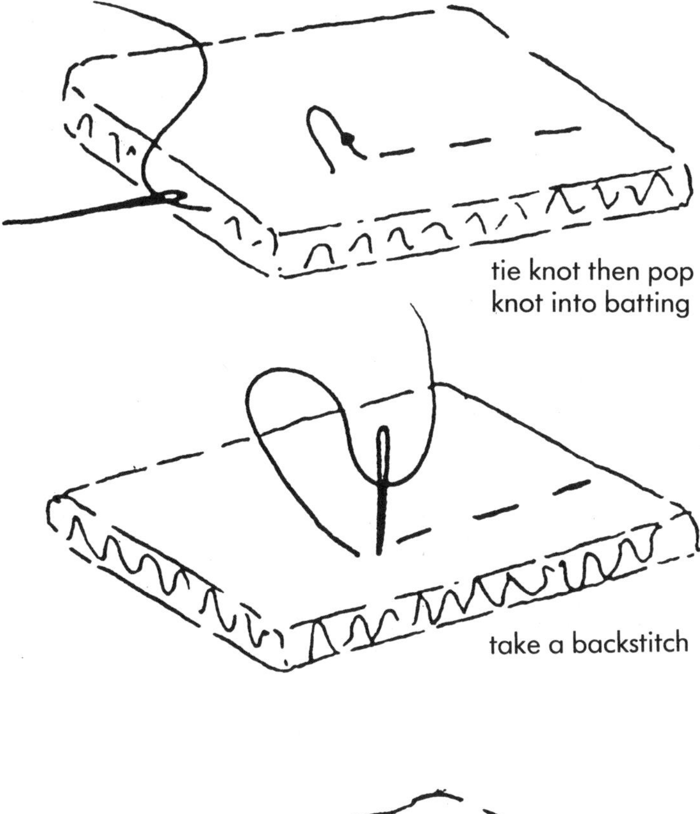

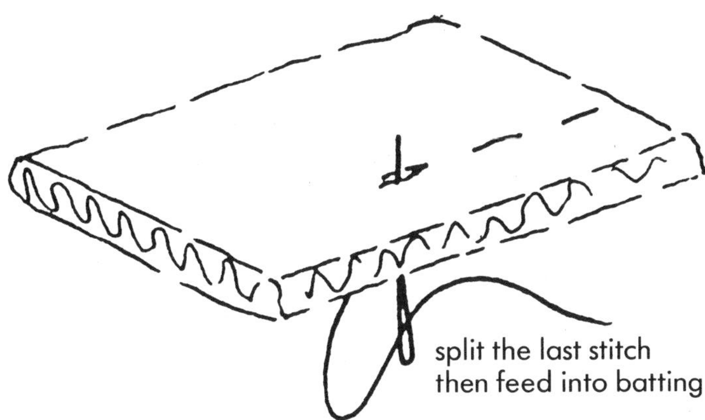

Figure 7.6

Whatever method of quilting you decide to use on your quilt, there are a couple of golden rules that should always be kept in mind.

Quilting must always be worked from the centre of the quilt outwards. This will keep the three layers of the quilt flat and smooth. I liken it to icing a cake — if you begin at the outside and work in, you end up with a lot of icing in the centre! Each time you move the hoop outwards, it should overlap a little of the quilting you have completed.

Don't leave more than a handspan unquilted. While the modern polyester batting does not require the fine close quilting that was needed in antique quilts filled with old blankets, worn clothes, etc., it is still wise not to leave more than about a 15 cm (6 inch) square without some sort of tying or quilting.

Binding The Quilt

This is the last task, after all the quilting is completed. Binding strips can be cut on the straight grain of fabric, unless your quilt has curved edges, in which case bias strips will be required. However, even straight-cut bindings, if they need to be joined, should be joined on the bias — this is less bulky.

Cut binding strips 8-12 cm (3-5 inches) wide, depending on the width of binding required, and the seam allowance to be used (i.e. four times the finished width of the binding, plus twice the seam allowance). Fold the strip in half lengthwise (right sides out). Cut two strips the exact length of the quilt. Place one on top of one long side of the quilt, matching raw edges. Sew on through all layers (here again a walking foot on your machine is useful). Trim off the batting and quilt back to the finished width of the binding. (Figure 7.7)

Figure 7.7

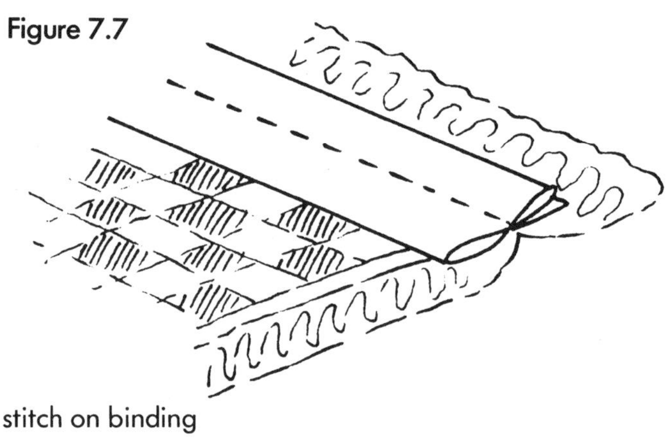

stitch on binding

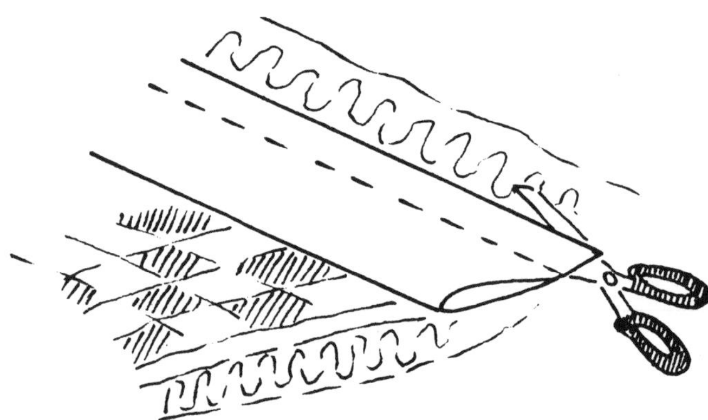

trim off excess batting

Turn the folded edge of the binding over to the back of the quilt and slip-stitch down along the machine stitching line. (Figure 7.8)

front of quilt

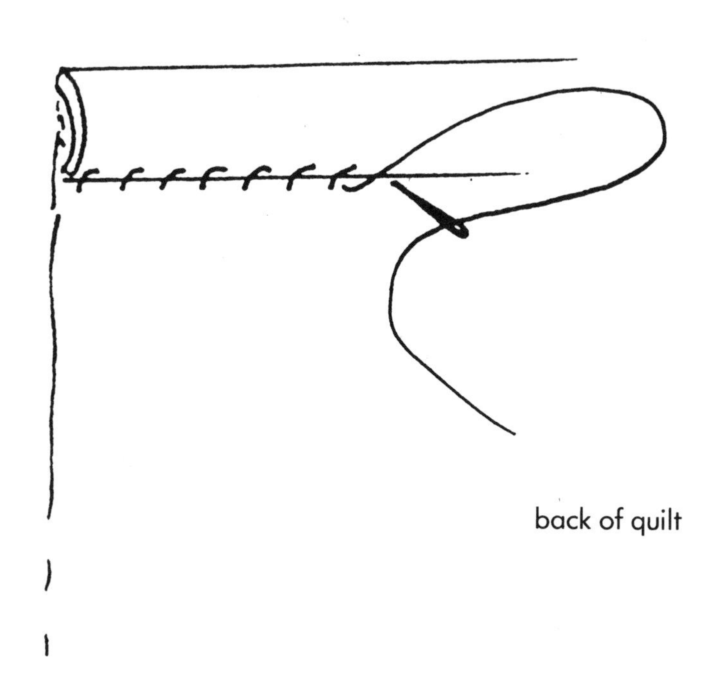

back of quilt

Figure 7.8

Repeat the process for the other long side. Cut two more strips of binding for the top and bottom (short) sides of the quilt. These should measure a little longer than the quilt edge, so that the raw ends can be turned in. Apply these bindings in the same way.

The back of the quilt can also be used as a binding, if the fabric suits you. Stitch through all layers by machine, as before, and trim the batting only back to the width of binding you require. Now bring the fabric from the back of the quilt to the front, tucking in raw edges and slip-stitching to the quilt front. (Figure 7.9)

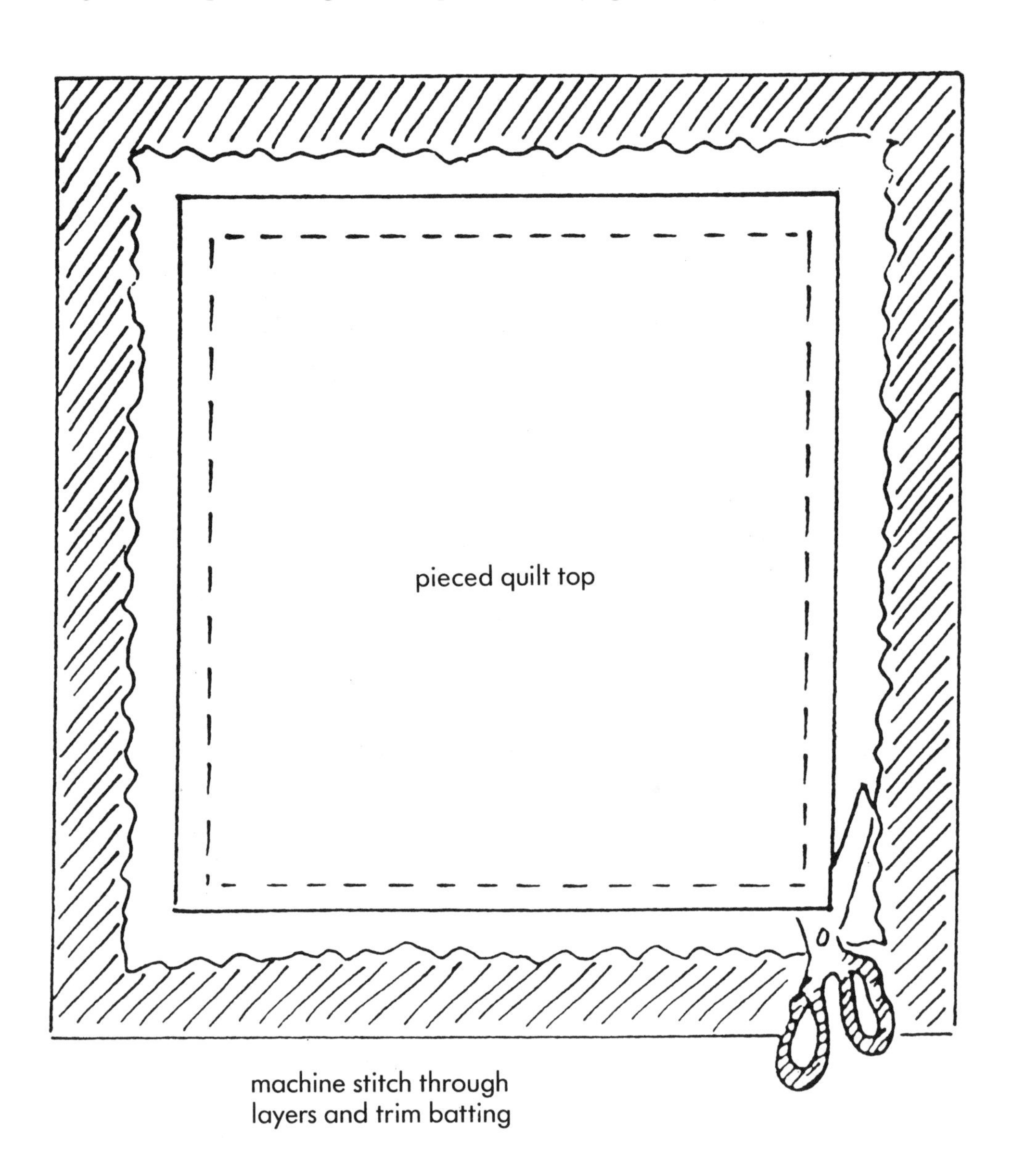

machine stitch through
layers and trim batting

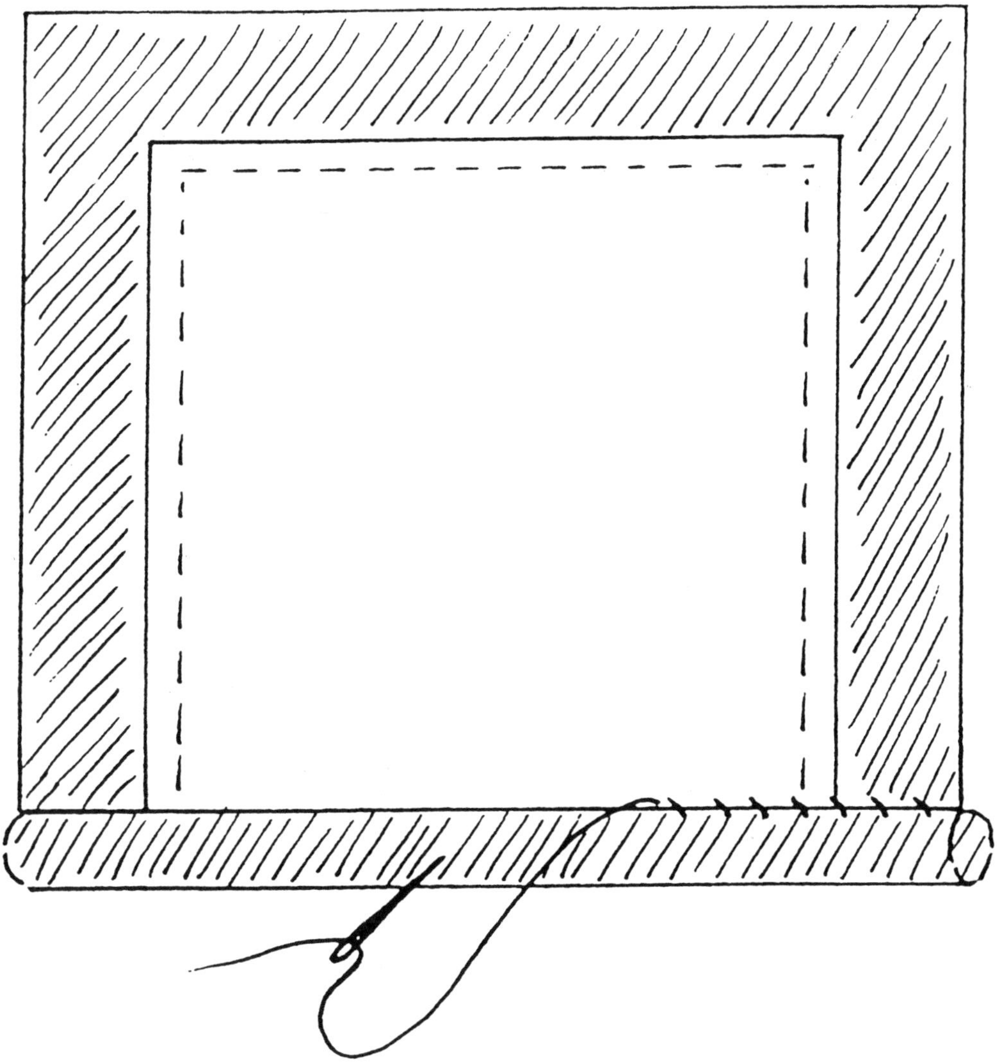

turn under raw edges, bring
back over and slip-stitch
to front

Figure 7.9

Other books in the Sally Milner Craft Series

Silk Ribbon Embroidery for Gifts and Garments
Jenny Bradford

Bullion Stitch Embroidery from Roses to Wildflowers
Jenny Bradford

Beautiful Boxes to Create, Cover and Decorate
Judy Newman

Cross Stitch Cards and Keepsakes
Jo Verso

The Embroiderer's Garden
Thomasina Beck

The Applique Book
Rose Verney

Traditional Embroidered Animals
Sarah Don